D1603592

Other Voices, Other Rooms

To Norm,
fellow poet
and friend
for years of
friendship

Tim

Other Voices, Other Rooms

Poems

TIM VIVIAN

Preface by Pamela Cranston

RESOURCE *Publications* · Eugene, Oregon

OTHER VOICES, OTHER ROOMS
Poems

Resource Publications
An Imprint of Wipf and Stock Publishers
199 W. 8th Ave., Suite 3
Eugene, OR 97401

www.wipfandstock.com

PAPERBACK ISBN: 978-1-7252-5867-9
HARDCOVER ISBN: 978-1-7252-5868-6
EBOOK ISBN: 978-1-7252-5869-3

Manufactured in the U.S.A.   02/21/20

With thanksgiving to the poets of my youth

E. E. Cummings
Richard Eberhart
T.S. Eliot
Stanley Kunitz
Robert Lowell
Howard Nemerov
Theodore Roethke
David Wagoner
Richard Wilbur
William Carlos Williams
James Wright

Midrash, pl. Midrashim
Hebrew: "interpretation, study,"
rabbinic Bible interpretation,
(1) an interpretation of a single verse of Scripture,
(2) a compilation of exegeses of Scripture,
(3) the method of exegesis characteristic of rabbinic Judaism.

—JONATHAN Z. SMITH, ED., THE HARPERCOLLINS DICTIONARY OF RELIGION, 717

"Now this is an allegory: these women are two covenants."

—GALATIANS 4:24

"I cannot say what poetry is; I know that our suffering and our concentrated joy, our states of plunging far and dark and turning to come back to the world . . . all are here . . . and there is an exchange here in which our lives are met, and created."

—MURIEL RUKEYSER

Contents

Preface

"It belongs to the imperfection of everything human that man can attain his desire only by passing through its opposite."

—Søren Kierkegaard, *The Journals*[1]

"To arrive where you are, to get from where you are not,
You must go by a way wherein there is no ecstasy.
In order to arrive at what you do not know
You must go by a way which is the way of ignorance."

—T.S. Eliot, "East Coker" in *The Four Quartets*[2]

I FIRST ENCOUNTERED TIM Vivian's poetry between 1985 and 1988, when we were seminary students studying for the Episcopal priesthood at the Church Divinity School of the Pacific in Berkeley, California. Though both of us had been writing poetry separately for many years, for my part, I shared my poems only with a chosen few. Tim was one of them, and he was always unfailingly supportive. When he sent me his brave first collection of poems for publication, asking me to write a preface for the book, I was delighted to do so. As I read them, I was riveted by his use of raw, powerful images and his acute perceptions, which I found gripping.

In "Mary's Gift to Gabriel (pp. 1-2), the first poem of Vivian's brilliant collection of poems, he writes:

> We've slung our beliefs into a ditch
> and called them detritus—or worse.

1. Søren Kierkegaard, *The Journals*, ed. and trans. Alexander Dru (London: Oxford University Press, 1938 (repr. 1959)), 90.

2. T.S. Eliot, "East Coker," *Four Quartets*, in Eliot, *The Complete Poems and Plays 1909–1950* (New York: Harcourt, Brace, 1971), 127.

But the depths of each slinging have
become feathers on the wings of each angel.
The angels now gather together,
bearing their burdens. Many can barely
fly.

Thus begins *Other Voices, Other Rooms*. The poems carry us into a deeply enfleshed, imagined world of Scripture. Of this collection, Vivian's "Mary's Gift to Gabriel" is to me the most beautiful and numinous poem in the book. It is the lamp by which we see all the others.

You might expect an Episcopal priest and professor emeritus of Religious Studies at California State University Bakersfield who teaches courses in Western and Indigenous Religions, who is an expert in the New Testament and Patristics, and who most notably is a scholar of the Desert Fathers and Mothers of fourth- to sixth-century monasticism, to write comforting and comfortable stories. This is not the case. These are complex, challenging, sophisticated, nuanced, deeply incarnational, dark, and earthy poems. Vivian uses story, theology, and history as a lens to look at Scripture of the Old and New Testament (and a bit of the Quran) from a new angle—and ourselves and our twenty-first-century world as well. It is not a pretty picture. That said, almost everything in these poems, for better or for worse, is written in hindsight with the events of the life, death, and resurrection of Jesus Christ as already having occurred. Thus, the Good News of the Gospel serves as a kind of backward-looking mirror and quiet undercurrent for both the narrators of the poems and those who read them.

This is not the first time that the midrash form has been used in a poetic context. The poet Scott Cairns uses it in his prose-poem commentary entitled "The Recovered Midrashim of Rabbi Sab" published in his 1998 collection *Recovered Body*. (A renowned poet, Cairns was originally ordained as a Presbyterian elder but in more recent years has found a spiritual home within the Syriac Orthodox Church.)

To explain further, Cairns discusses the origins of the word midrash in an interview published in the journal *Prairie Schooner*. Midrash, he tells us, "derives from the Hebrew verb *d'rash*, to seek out. So, one might say that the *Darshan* (the writer of midrash) employs strategies of close reading and invention in order to search out subtle possibilities of meaning from sacred passages."[3] Cairns said he created Rabbi Sab as a partly-

3. Scott Cairns and Gregory Dunne, "A Conversation with Scott Cairns," *Prairie*

fictional character to embody the combined aspects of historical Jewish and Christian figures such as Sabbatai Zevi, Isaac Luria, Abba Simeon, St. Ephraim the Syrian, St. Isaac the Syrian, St. Athanasius, and Origen among others, to give voice to his midrash.

Unlike Cairns, Tim Vivian has not created a fictional Rabbi as a literary device for his poetic interpretations, but rather has made himself a *Darshan*, a writer of midrash. His use of the first-person narrative creates an immediacy that brings the reader inside the scene. The effect is striking and frankly sometimes shocking.

In these poems, good men are hard to find. The corrupt and cynical cast of characters the reader encounters in these poems includes Pilate, Herod, Judas, Adam and Cain, David and Bathsheba, Barabbas—the insurrectionist pardoned by Pilate at Passover on Good Friday—and Satan himself. Jesus, of course, stands with the good: the Virgin Mary, Mary of Magdala, Lazarus, St. Peter, St. Stephen, deacon and martyr, a compassionate Roman soldier, and the unnamed faithful male and female disciples. There is goodness here, but most of these poems are written from the warped perspective of those who trample goodness and distort it.

This slanted perspective is not new among Christian writers. As the short story writer Flannery O'Connor famously writes:

> Writers who see by the light of their Christian faith will have, in these times, the sharpest eye for the grotesque, for the perverse, and for the unacceptable . . . When you can assume that your audience holds the same beliefs you do, you can relax a little and use more normal means of talking to it; when you have to assume that it does not, then you have to make your vision apparent by shock—to the hard of hearing you shout, and for the almost-blind you draw large and startling figures.[4]

Vivian's poems are startling—they are not an easy read. Sometimes the reader has to dig for the meaning, working hard as a miner digging for diamonds—but it is well worth the effort. When the reader does the necessary work, he or she will discover breathtaking poems such as "Mary's Gift to Gabriel" (1-2), "They Wept" (23-24), "Crown of Thorns" (46-48), "The Presence of the LORD" (43-45), "We at Great Distance" (56), and "Those Who Now See" (3-4).

Schooner 79.1 (Spring 2005) 44–52; 51.

4. Flannery O'Connor, "The Fiction Writer and His Country," in *Mystery and Manners: Occasional Prose*, ed. Sally and Robert Fitzgerald (New York: Farrar, Straus & Giroux, 1969), 33–34.

To enter the world of these poems is to become like one who is blind—either one born blind or one who prefers to turn a blind eye toward evil and suffering in the world but is forced to look at it anyway. These poems are as compelling and brutal as the irresistible pull that compels rubberneckers to watch the remains of a car crash on the freeway: one keeps reading and watching anyway.

"Those Who Now See" (3-4) is a midrash on the passage in John 9:1–12 where Jesus heals the man born blind. In John's Gospel, Jesus answers the essential question: "Who sinned? This man, or his parents?" In Vivian's version, the answer goes like this:

> John's Gospel records one
> answer. But there are many.
> Jesus picks up a flower that
> someone has dropped in the
> street. Placing it on the blind
> man's tongue, he now kisses
> the pleading man's each eye.
> When the blind eyes open,
> Jesus takes the flower and
> walks it into a household
> garden where he removes
> all the petals. Planting them,
> he will return the next day,
> assured, to see each seed a
> flower, those who now see.

Like the blind man healed by Jesus, readers of these poems will receive a new vision—one they cannot forget. This is what any good work of art hopes to do—to be unforgettable.

In his Author's Note, Tim Vivian hopes "that each reader of these poems will read, and reread, himself or herself into, and out from, the poems. Perhaps some, or lines of some, can inform lectio, reflective reading" (xx-xxi). The author wants the reader to take his poems personally. As the Collect in the Book of Common Prayer invites us to do, we are asked "to read, mark, learn, and inwardly digest." It takes effort to dig down into Vivian's collection, into the dark, into ourselves. His poems act like mirrors making us confront sin and separation from God in ourselves—and in the world.

Depending upon our stance and our honesty as we approach these unsettling poems, we may come away either shriven or humbled and comforted. Once we put the book down and resurface to resume the routine of our daily lives of work, traffic, grocery lists, and the chaos of the current US political climate, we will discover that we've become, by necessity, blinded by a new light.

Pamela Cranston
Oakland, California
Feast of St. Edmund, King and Martyr

Author's Note

THE ENGLISH WORD "STORY" comes from Greek *historía* which, at its root, means "inquiry, research," "result of research, information, knowledge," "telling, exposition, account, history." Its cognate verb *historéō* makes verbal these nouns: "to seek to know oneself, inform oneself, do research, inquire," "interrogate," "examine, explore, observe." *Historía*, smiling, sits side-by-side on a vernal park bench with the Delphic Oracle's "Know thyself." *Historía* later came to mean "to come to know or inform oneself through history."[1] All history is story. All of the definitions above are apposite to the poems in this volume.

As Deborah Miranda, quoting Leslie Silko, tells us, "Stories are 'all we have' . . . And it is true. Human beings have no other way of knowing that we exist, or what we have survived, except through the vehicle of story."[2] Miranda continues: "Story is the most powerful force in the world . . . Story is culture. Story, like culture, is constantly moving. It is a river where no gallon of water is the same gallon it was one second ago. Yet it is the same river. It exists as a truth. As a whole. Even if the whole is in constant change. In fact, *because* of that constant change."[3] Stories, we need to remember, do not come only with words, or sounds: the Lascaux cave paintings are as much as 20,000 years old.

In Religious Studies, my academic discipline, the term "myth," sacred story, has nothing negative about it; in fact, myth is proclamation, revelation, and instruction, oftentimes difficult, oftentimes delightful, often both.[4] Many of the poems here deal with difficult subjects, but we

1. *The Brill Dictionary of Ancient Greek*, ed. Franco Montanari, English eds. Madeleine Goh and Chad Schroeder (Leiden: Brill, 2015), 991c.

2. Miranda, *Bad Indians: A Tribal Memoir* (Berkeley, CA: Heyday, 2013), xi.

3. Miranda, *Bad Indians*, xvi; emphasis hers.

4. For a good, accessible introduction, see Eva M. Thury and Margaret K. Devinney, *Introduction to Mythology: Contemporary Approaches to Classical and World*

all know in our lives that we need to, or should, deal with difficulties. The basic meaning of Islam's *jihād* is "struggle," usually in the Qur'ān (Koran) a spiritual struggle within. As Pamela Cranston aptly says in her Preface, the storytelling here often has "slant."

"Slant," in my understanding, bears with it hope. I take heart from the hope that is the life-giving heart of *all* religious traditions. The poet Kathleen Raine makes a very important point about T. S. Eliot's "The Wasteland," his poetic contemplation on the world after World War I, the horrific "war to end all wars." Eliot, she emphasizes, "has shown us what the world is very apt to forget, that the statement of a terrible truth has a kind of healing power. In his stern vision of the hell that lies about us . . . , there is a quality of grave consolation. In his statement of the worst, Eliot has always implied the whole extent of the reality of which the worst is only one part."[5] Eliot himself concludes "The Wasteland" with "Shantih shantih shantih."[6] "Grave consolation": very often the very definition of myth—and, I hope, of the poems in this volume.

At its root, "myth," even confrontational myth, means "sacred story." In Western religion(s) the stories of the patriarchs and matriarchs, the actions and parables of Jesus, stories in the Qur'ān, hadith about Muhammad; in Eastern religions, the spiritual journey(s) of the Buddha and the melodious cacophony of the Hindu pantheon; worldwide, the origins and trickster stories of Indigenous peoples like the Lakota Sioux. These myths, these stories, convey to their readers sacred truths. Myth, story, very often becomes ritual (Passover, Hanukkah; Ramadan, the Hajj; Christmas, Easter). Stories embrace metaphor, and metaphors befriend story. Metaphor is the flow of blood giving life to story. Without it, scriptural stories (see, for example the Prophets and Jesus) cannot even draw breath. As David Bentley Hart says, "the language of Scripture is full of metaphor, on just about every page . . ."[7]

Myths, fourth ed. (New York: Oxford University Press, 2017).

5. Cited by Wendell Berry, "The Way of Ignorance," in *Wendell Berry: Essays 1993–2017*, ed. Jack Shoemaker (New York: The Library of America, 2019), 377–99; 389 (source not given).

6. Eliot, "The Wasteland," in Eliot, *The Complete Poems and Plays*, 50. Eliot's n. 434 (p. 55): "Shantih [Shanti]. Repeated as here, a formal ending to an Upanishad. 'The Peace which passeth understanding' is a feeble translation of the conduct of this word."

7. Hart, *That All Shall be Saved: Heaven, Hell, and Universal Salvation* (New Haven: Yale University Press, 2019), 94. He says this as part of his riposte to "infernalists" (his word), biblical "literalists" who champion everlasting fire and brimstone. I would add that the very nature of language tells us that there is, really, no such thing as "literalism."

Such stories, all stories, ask for—even demand—attentive listening, interpretation, and reinterpretation. But reflection must come before interpretation, and reinterpretation. Middle French *réflexion* comes into English *as* "reflection, refleccion, reflexion," "the action of bending or turning back, action of reflecting (light, etc.)."[8] Thus, we turn our attention both back to the text and to ourselves. The author-editors of Deuteronomy in the Hebrew Bible (Christian Old Testament) rework Leviticus; in the first century CE the Gospel writers interpret the Jesus of received tradition differently for different audiences (for example, for the writer of Matthew's Gospel and his Jewish audience, Jesus is the new Moses); in his letter to the Galatians (4:21–31) Paul allegorizes (he employs the verb) the story of Sarah and Hagar from the Hebrew Bible (Genesis 16 and 18); the early rabbis bring forth the Talmud, rabbinic interpretations, and disagreements, concerning Scripture; followers of Jesus in the second and third centuries write additional, usually supersessionist, Gospels and Acts. Islam's Tafsir, commentaries, midrash the Qur'ān. Every person of faith since who comes to these Scriptures "takes and reads" (the voice's command to Saint Augustine: *Tolle, lege*; "Take, read").

One such "reader" was the Italian painter Caravaggio (1571–1610), who is relevant here. Mario Dal Bello points out Caravaggio's "apparently strong preference for Biblical subjects, as well as his detailed, continuous preoccupation with a number of major themes from the Old and New Testaments."[9] When I was in Rome a little before this book went to press, I was able to view Caravaggio's "The Calling of Saint Matthew" at the Church of San Luigi dei Francesi. I saw that Caravaggio is doing in paint what I'm attempting with words. As Dal Bello puts it: Caravaggio "emphasizes a number of specific aspects of the texts, constructs them in stages of a visual commentary . . . , and makes them relevant to daily life."[10]

With "The Calling of Saint Matthew" (1599–1600) Caravaggio *reimagines*, *reinterprets*, a very brief biblical story: "As Jesus was walking along, he saw a man called Matthew sitting at the tax booth; and he said to him, 'Follow me.' And he got up and followed him."[11] One sentence.

8. *Oxford English Dictionary* online, https://www.oed.com/view/Entry/160921?redirectedFrom=reflection#eid.

9. Mario Dal Bello, *The Bible of Caravaggio: Images from the Old and New Testament* (Regensburg, Germany: Schnell & Steiner, 2017), 13.

10. Dal Bello, 13.

11. Matt 9:9//Mark 2:14//Luke 5:2.

But a very loaded one: Matthew is a hated tax collector (more accurately, a tax farmer, who gets a cut beyond the already-oppressive Roman taxes). The Gospel account then continues with two very important sentences, sentences not emphasized but ones that tell us a great deal about Jesus and his ministry: "And as [Jesus] sat at dinner in the house, many tax collectors and sinners came and were sitting with him and his disciples. When the Pharisees saw this, they said to his disciples, 'Why does your teacher eat with tax collectors and sinners?'" In Dal Bello's words, here is Caravaggio's depiction of Matthew's call, replete with details imagined out from, and into, the Gospel account:

> In a tavern, where men are playing dice, Christ suddenly appears with a ray of light (grace) from an unseen window where Matthew hesitates, while various light fragments extract other figures from the shadows . . . Caravaggio describes the world of those who are either not called upon or remain indifferent to grace [and those called and not indifferent]. An astonishingly diverse human comedy ensues."[12]

This is "comedy" (and tragedy) as in Dante's *Divine Comedy*. Caravaggio has reimagined the Biblical scene for us, one that is still very relevant more than 400 years later. He then invites us into the painting and, thus, into ourselves.

Each person, therefore, whether painter or poet, attentive observer or reader, *becomes* translator and interpreter, speaking in tongues (so to speak), an exegete, a proclaimer, even if only for herself or himself. The midrashim here are such explorations, taking scriptural stories that they imagine, and reimagine, in order to offer the reader different angles and perspectives, new experiences. Again, Eliot:

> We shall not cease from exploration
> And the end of all our exploring
> Will be to arrive where we started
> And know the place for the first time.[13]

My hope is that each reader of these poems, each explorer, will read, and reread, himself or herself into, and out from, the poems. Perhaps some, or lines of some, even a word, can inform *lectio*, reflective reading. Kathleen Norris puts it very well: "*Lectio* is an attempt to read more with

---

12. Dal Bello, 53.

13. T. S. Eliot, "Little Gidding," *The Complete Poems and Plays*, 145.

the heart than with the head. One does not try to 'cover' a certain amount of material so much as surrender to whatever word or phrase catches the attention. A slow, meditative reading . . . respects the power of words to resonate with the full range of human experience." [14]

My area of research is early Christian monasticism, and in that literature, mostly stories (even the *apophthegmata*, sayings, are stories in miniature), the numerous, even vast numbers of, scriptural allusions usually go unnoted in translations and, hence, unnoticed by many readers. Thus, we lose vital scriptural context and contour that give us information for transformation. Notes there are essential.[15] Different from most books of poetry, this volume supplies footnotes to many of the poems with brief glosses that explain and/or inform about certain terms or provide sources for scriptural allusions.

A suggestion: before reading a poem, the reader may first want to look at the notes so she or he has extra food for the journey, reading them in tandem with the poem. I ask (well, tell) my students that when they're reading they should have their phones handy so they can use the web to look up people, places, and words. The notes here do some of that seeking and finding. My mantra for my students when they're studying—well, anything—is "Context, Context, Context." The notes with the poems provide at least partial context. Perhaps the greatest abuse of scripture now is reading—and, especially, proof texting—it without its context, which means, really, without its consent, or content.

This volume also supplies a Scripture Index at the end for those who want to look up a passage in Scripture and find the poem or poems that employ it, either in the text or in the notes.

I have used throughout "Hebrew Bible" for the Jewish Scriptures rather than the supersessionist "Old Testament" of Christianity.

I have done my best to use inclusive language. We students and readers always need to remember that what we call "inclusive language" was not a concern of the ancients (or even of our parents and grandparents). When I imagine these folks thinking or speaking, they often use language we would not.

The terms "BCE" (Before Common Era) and "CE" (Common Era) are more-inclusive scholarly terms for "BC" and "AD," respectively.

14. Norris, *The Cloister Walk* (NY: Riverhead Books, 1996), xx.

15. See Tim Vivian, *A Participated Light: The Saying and Stories of the Desert Fathers and Mothers*, vol. 1 (Collegeville, MN: Cistercian, forthcoming 2021). Eliot supplies over 400 notes for "The Wasteland."

All references to and citations from the Bible, unless otherwise noted, are to the New Revised Standard Version (NRSV).

I have followed the practice of the NRSV in using LORD when Jews speak of or to God. LORD, "Adonai," stands in for YHWH, the Sacred Name that Jews, out of respect, did not and do not pronounce (Exodus 3:13–15). The Septuagint (the third-c. BCE Greek translation of the Hebrew Bible, which all the New Testament authors use) uses Greek *kýrios*; "Lord," without all caps, is what the first Christians used for Jesus. But we need to remember that the *kýrios* they heard and enunciated symbolled and sounded both "LORD," God, and "the Lord," Jesus/Christ, thus providing a linguistic theology.

The symbol "//" indicates parallel passages within the Gospels, especially between Matthew, Mark, and Luke, the "Synoptic" Gospels.

To so many people I offer thanks, but especially to the people of Grace-St. Paul's (2007–2017) who supported me during *our* ten years of mutual, and prophetic, ministry.

Deep thanks to The Rev. Pamela Cranston, fellow seminarian and poet, for her prayers, encouragement, writing the Preface, helping me with publishing matters, and for her many thoughtful suggestions.

My thanks also to my son David Vivian for his suggestions, and The Rev. Gary Commins ("Coach"), dear friend of many years, who read through the proofs.

My thanks to Miriam, for her support, in so many ways, of her backyard hermit.

Thanks, too, to Gwen Hardage-Vergeer, the first reader of many of these poems, for her constant encouragement.

And thanks to my doctoral professor Apostolos Athanassakis for etymological corroborations and to my university colleague Mark Lamas for our numerous discussions of things biblical and Roman, for his information and insights.

Finally, my thanks to the good folks at Wipf & Stock.

Tim Vivian
All Saints' Day, 2019
tvivian@csub.edu

MARY'S GIFT TO GABRIEL

A Midrash on Luke 1:26–38

We've slung our beliefs into a ditch
and called them detritus—or worse.[1]
But the depths of each slinging have
become feathers on the wings of each

angel. The angels now gather together,
bearing their burdens. Many can barely
fly. Raphael, weighed down, is one—
this is why in Scripture we so seldom

see him.[2] Many of the angels can fly no
longer: these the Devil's minions cart
off to convalescent homes from which
nothing of value will ever come, only

cardboard boxes wide enough for
folded wings. God weeps continually
over these failures, the Godhead's,
and ours. But these our angels still

in flight carry passports, each with
Gabriel's image. The belief, still
strong, is that he, while a fledgling,
once visited Mary. But before she

1. Beliefs: Greek singular *pístis*. In the Greek of the New Testament, and the concomitant theology, *pístis* means "faith," and the verb *pisteúō* means to have faith, trust *in* something or someone. It is, then, communal, rather than doctrinal and/or individualistic. Walter Bauer, Frederick W. Danker, W. F. Arndt, and F. W. Gingrich, eds., *Greek-English Lexicon of the New Testament and Other Early Christian Literature*, third ed. (Chicago: University of Chicago Press, 2000) [BDAG], 816a: "to consider something to be true and therefore worthy of one's trust, believe; believe in something, be convinced of something." "Belief" and "believe," then, do not make the claim that one must assent to propositions, an understanding common now.

2. Raphael . . . / in Scripture we so seldom / see him: the archangel Raphael ("God heals") appears only in Tobit, dated to 225–175 BCE.

welcomes him, she sits him down
and cleanses each feather deeply
burdened. Now that he can move
without pain, she is ready to listen.

THOSE WHO NOW SEE

A Midrash on John 9:1–12

Each leaf of every plant has
its own beauty. The dying
palm frond, self-ostracizing
from family and neighbors,

enemies and friends, now
leans far down, almost into
the neighboring vincas, each
flower its own Annunciation,

Birth and its Transfiguration,
Resurrection its Ascension.
Too much? Too little. Each
lambent pink flower has its

own raising of Lazarus,[3] its
giving of eyesight to the
man born blind. Before he
sees again, his arms around

the waist of Jesus, his tears
turning Jesus' cloak scarlet,
the people ask this no-one
from Galilee *Who sinned?*

This man, or his parents?
John's Gospel records one
answer. But there are many.
Jesus picks up a flower that

someone has dropped in the
street. Placing it on the blind
man's tongue, he now kisses
the pleading man's each eye.

---

3. Lazarus: John 11:1–44.

When the blind eyes open,
Jesus takes the flower and
walks it into a household
garden where he removes

each petal. Planting them,
he will return the next day,
assured, to see each seed a
flower, those who now see.[4]

4. Each seed a / flower: see Gen 26:12–14 and the Parable of the Sower (Matt 13:1–9//Mark 4:1–9//Luke 8:4–8).

IN DREAMS BEGIN RESPONSIBILITIES[5]

A Midrash on Amos 2:6 and 8:6

I once had a dream that an equinox
captured me: it gagged and bound me,
then shoved me into its cage. When I
asked *Where, then, can I find God's*

truth?[6] the equinox's prophets—who
are also its harbingers and seers—
told me that the holy prophet Amos
understood the difference between

cage and the cage's captivity. *These
prisons*, he warns, *we manufacture
each day, selling from within the
poor for a pair of sandals.* In dream,

beneath this equinox, I see thumbs
heavy on scales, choke-collars on our
slaves. Still within the dream, I now
see the dead, no longer bound, rise

from their graves in paupers's fields:
*What? Only now you ask? No, we
don't have hammers and scythes and
sickles with which to bludgeon and*

*dismember those who tortured us
into death.* I watch them move quietly.
They kneel to pray before the throne
of each person who murdered them.

---

5. In Dreams Begin Responsibilities: the title of a short story by Delmore Schwartz.

6. Truth: the word has a fascinating Greek family. *Léthe* means "oblivion," cognate with the verb *lanthánomai*, "to forget" and the Latin verb *lateo* (to hide). *Léthe* in mythology is the river that the dead must cross, ferried by Charon, to the other side. *Alétheia* is "non-oblivion." The "a" is an alpha-privative, a negative, as in "atypical" and "asymmetric." Thus "truth" etymologically means "not forgetting," not being "oblivious" or "in oblivion." See Hesiod, *Theogony* 26–28.

And now I see God opening a hostel.
Each room welcomes its honored guest.[7]

7. I see God opening a hostel. / Each room welcomes its honored guest: John 14:1–2.

THE BREAD AND THE WINE: A FOLLOWER, DEEP IN HIDING, TELLS HIS STORY

A Midrash on Matthew 27:1–2, 11–26;
Mark 15:1–15; Lk 23:1–25; John 18:28–40

I know my Greeks (well, some
of them). I bathe each day in
Periclean light.[8] I drink daily
from Socrates's cup—and live.

And for what? Unclean vermin
crawl all around and over me.
They slither out of my ears.
Truly, I fear what I feel now

in my anus and penis. I tremble.
I want to scream at my forsaking
Adonai. I swear, unless this my
suffering ends, and soon, I will

ask Plato whom, or what, I can
trust, believe in. I was a mere
sub-adjudicator during his trial;
always in hiding, I shuttled the

recriminations back and forth
between the Sanhedrin and these
filthy Romans.[9] When Pilate at
last deigned to appear before

8. Periclean light: Pericles (c. 495–29 BCE) was a prominent and influential Greek statesman, orator, and general of Athens during its golden age, specifically the time between the Persian and Peloponnesian wars.

9. Sanhedrin: Greek *synédrion,* "sitting together," hence "assembly" or "council." The word can indicate a "governing board, council," or "the high council in Jerusalem," the Sanhedrin.

us, the slave trailing his triumph[10]
carried a basin and wash pitcher,
the finest of soaps, and the most
eloquent of linens. Pilate held

us captive in sordid dramaturgy.
I do not think that anyone even
dared to breathe—except one.
Before the slave even finished

setting up, this one leapt forth,
sica withdrawn from his robes.[11]
But before he took two steps, a
Roman soldier (they are always

on the alert for assassination)
sprang forward, stabbed the one
deep into his breast and, even as
our one fell, disemboweled him.

Pilate, not for a moment losing
his sardonic smile, promised that
whole cohort the finest Falernian
wine that night.[12] He told the one

10. Triumph: A Roman triumph (*triumphus*) was a civil ceremony and religious rite of ancient Rome, held to publicly celebrate and sanctify the success of a military commander who had led Roman forces to victory in the service of the state or, originally and traditionally, one who had successfully completed a foreign war. On the day of his triumph, the general wore a crown of laurel and the all-purple, gold-embroidered, triumphal *toga picta* ("painted toga"), regalia that identified him as near-kingly or near-divine, and he was known to paint his face red. He rode in a four-horse chariot through the streets of Rome in unarmed procession with his army, captives, and the spoils of his victory. See Mary Beard, *The Roman Triumph*, and Google "the arch of Titus."

11. *Sica*, pl. *sicae*: the Sicarii were a splinter group of the Jewish Zealots who, in the decades preceding Jerusalem's destruction in 70 CE, violently opposed the Roman occupation of Judea and attempted to expel the Romans and their sympathizers. The Sicarii carried *sicae*, small daggers, concealed in their cloaks. At public gatherings, they pulled out these daggers to attack Romans and Israelite Roman sympathizers alike, blending into the crowd after the deed to escape detection.

12. Falernian wine: Latin *Falernum*, this wine became the most renowned wine produced in ancient Rome.

soldier that the next land that he
appropriated would be his, a gift
from our most illustrious and
noble *DIVI FILIUS*, Caesar.[13] The

soldier bowed and, alert, moved
closer to him. Pilate now nodded
to his slave to commence these
his ablutions. The slave poured

water, purified, into the basin.
Since the followers of this Jesus,
under torture, have confessed to
us, said Pilate, *I will begin to*

wash my hands. Now Rome's
governor motioned us with his
eyes, without a word, into a line
such as wretched slaves form

at the auction block. But not one
of us moved. So Pilate nodded
to that one soldier. He withdrew
his weapon, still bloody, from its

scabbard. Pilate commanded
him to hold the sword out, flat
towards us. The governor now
looks at me as I try to shrink

into saving obscurity. Yes, Your
Eminence, I reply. *I command*
you: Kiss this bloodied sword
and then come forward to wash

13. DIVI FILIUS: Son of God, a term Roman emperors used of themselves and put
on their coins. John Dominic Crossan and Richard A. Horsley have shown how Paul
subverts Roman imperial-religious language by applying some of its terms to Christ.
In his Gospel, Mark does the same with the triumph, the "anti-triumph" of Jesus' "tri-
umphal" entry into Jerusalem. See n. 10.

your hands. You will do both. If
we find blood on your lips, or
if you wash your hands and in
that washing the water turns

crimson, we will—no, be calm—
we will not crucify you, like him
whom you call Messiah, King
and Savior. We will command

you—all hail to glorious Caesar—
to take the bread he has called
his body and the wine he has
termed his blood (his followers

have told us of this), to take them,
first the bread, and eat, and then
the wine, and drink. We know who
you are. Do this and you will live.

ONLY ONE FOLLOWS HIM

A Midrash on Luke 4:3

"When the Devil had finished every test
[or: temptation],[14] he departed from [Jesus]
until an opportune time."

Adam's curse,[15] they raise clouds as Roman
chariots do careening through our captive
streets. But amid these thronging billows
I see—I swear, I do not lie, nor am I mad—

I see Jesus among them, unhelmeted.[16] I see
him, without reins, riding on a borrowed
donkey.[17] Wearing a peasant's mean tatters,
he nevertheless looks only forward, always

in command. But in command of what? Only
with my questions do I realize that this is
a Roman triumph, without victims and victors,
never seen in Galilee, or Jerusalem.[18] We have

heard of them, distant. But there is no proud
soldiery with him, no multitudes of bound and
chained prisoners of war awaiting death, or its
identical twin, slavery. Only one follows him.

14. Test: or "temptation": Greek *peirasmós*.

15. Adam's curse: Gen 3:17–19. "Clouds" and "billows" are allusions to "clouds of *dust*"; see Gen 2:7 and 3:19, which have an etymological wordplay between "Adam" and *adama*, "earth." *The Anchor Bible Dictionary*, ed. David Noel Freedman (New York: Doubleday, 1992) I.62b, says that the etymology is uncertain; it correctly notes that "word plays in themselves do not necessarily indicate the etymology of a word."

16. I see Jesus among them: Matt 21:1–11//Mark 11:1–11//Luke 19:28–40//John 12:12–19.

17. Riding on a borrowed / donkey: Matt 21:1–5; John 12:14–15.

18. Roman triumph: see n. 10.

Crowned, berobed, sceptered, and wearing
golden raiment, he nevertheless crawls behind,
impossibly fast, eating Adam's remains. When
he spots me, Satan laughs, and lunges for me.

THERE ARE, SOMETIMES, CIRCUMSTANCES: ADAM, EAST OF EDEN, REFLECTS

A Midrash on 1 Corinthians 15:21–22

"For since death came through a
human being, the resurrection of
the dead has also come through
a human being; for as all die in
Adam, so all will be made alive
in Christ."

There are, sometimes, circumstances
beyond Death's control, as when Jesus,[19]
not the Romans, hammered himself to
the accursèd tree we had planted long

ago when we fled east of Eden.[20] I was
still overwhelmed by her naked beauty.
Why only then—I still ask myself—
why only then did I understand God's

truth: the knowledge, wisdom, insight,
compassion, and justice that informed
her presence? The dust she raised with
each bare footfall?[21] In the east, I breathed

in things unfinished until I could breathe
no more. It was only then, only then,
when she saw me struggling for each
breath, that she handed me the hammer.

19. Jesus . . . / hammered himself to / the accursèd tree we had planted / long ago
when we fled east of Eden: see Gen 2:9; 3:24; Deut 21:22–23.

20. East of Eden: Gen 3:24.

21. Dust: see Gen 2:7; 3:14, 19; see n. 15.

13

SATAN NODS BACK INTO SLEEP

A Midrash on Zechariah 3:1–5

I brought you with me, once, into
stone. But stone was not what you
wanted. You wanted, you said, the
white remembrance of bone, its

memories, its regrets, its maculate
nightmares and their nocturnal
enemies. Why we—not just you—
desire these things occupies one

corner—no, a slightest fragment
of Adonai's dismays and losses.
Each morning, the LORD gathers
the shavings, the rats's droppings,

from around the bed. With care,
the LORD places them now within
the burial shroud always kept near.
As Kaddish resounds, the day's

sun, the night's moon, these our
auspicious yet war-palsied faces,
gather to dance.[22] As the psaltery
begins, Satan nods back into sleep.

---

22. Auspicious: divination and augury were important practices in Antiquity. As
with *haruspex* (see n. 82), English "auspicious" comes from Latin via French, Latin *aus-*
picium: "a bird-watching, divination from flight of birds." The nominative singular of
auspic- is *auspex*, as in *haruspex*.

BETWEEN EACH LETTER: A MONTH AFTER THE CRUCIFIXION AND RESURRECTION

A Midrash on Matthew 6:19–21

Our intermittent praises once sanctified spirits.
Not spirits whose souls, birthed by Spirit,[23] were
God's flesh and blood and bone, but wraiths
that now are voids, both outside and deep within.

There wanders Herod, alone.[24] Over there—there—
staggers our Pilate, off balance, because he dare
not search for the home of his exile, in some
near-barbarian land where sheep beg for mercy

before their slaughter.[25] Wreathed, intinctured red
now brown by the spirit gushing from dead men's
throats, he still commands all those doing Rome's
licit slaughter: crucifixions and dismemberments.

Herod, indifferent to gore and mayhem, chortles
a voiceless laugh, one mottled by moth and rust.[26]
He says *I would rather wander, even indwell,*
these Judean deserts than kiss the bloodied feet

of their peasant, crucified, god. When we hear his
maledictions, we, now terrified, once again sing
his praises. But now they bear no sound, no syllable:
between each letter hangs our Lord and Savior.

---

23. Spirit: Greek *pneûma*, like Hebrew *ruah*, means "breath," "wind," and "spirit."

24. Herod: Herod Antipas, Tetrarch of Galilee and Peraea 4 BCE–39 CE.

25. Pilate . . . / the home of his exile: after his prefecture ended in 36–37 CE, Pilate was summoned back to Rome, but there is no historical record of his life after that.

26. Moth and rust: Matt 6:19–20.

NAILS LIKE MANNA:
AFTER THE CRUCIFIXION
AND RESURRECTION

The hollowing out of skin is yet
skin—until you reach flesh's
bone. Even then what remains
of skin, become blood, assures

us that help is at hand, surgery
will save, and healing will give
both death and its resurrection.
You can, if you dare to believe,

watch it—I mean both—happen.
No, it—I mean they—do not occur
at once: resurrection must come
first. Only then will death begin

its slow march backwards, scythe
in each hand, cowering beneath now-
unafraid derisions and catcalls. Our
crucified will eat nails like manna.[27]

27. Manna: see Exod 16:31–35.

BELONGING TO THE VISION IS THE VISION

A Midrash on Revelation 1

Why have you come, all the way to Patmos,
to see me?[28] Some accept the Apocalypse,
some don't.[29] Besides, the Roman Empire
still stands. The younger Pliny,[30] that wise

idolater, asks Emperor Trajan[31] if he, Pliny,
can murder Christians if they refuse three
times to renounce their crimes. These
crimina, of course, Pliny never specifies.

So why have you come all this way to visit
an old, old man whose dreams and visions
have come to nothing? Your answer is kind,
but insufficient. Here last night I had yet

another vision. Want to hear it? I saw three
stars in God's vast and inescapable heavens.
I ran, and ran, but could not outrun them.
They followed me to Rome. Vespasian still

sat the throne.[32] When I asked the vision why
an idolater some thirty years ago appeared,
it prophesied to me: *Vespasian, Trajan, they
are all the same. Tiberius never even heard*

---

28. Patmos: see Rev 1:9. Patmos is a small Greek island in the Aegean Sea.

29. Some accept the Apocalypse / some don't: "apocalypse" in Greek is *apokálypsis*, an "uncovering," especially an uncovering of something hidden, hence Latin *revelatio*, "revelation," as in "reveal." Some early Christian communities did not accept Revelation as canonical.

30. Pliny: Pliny the Younger (61–c. 113 CE). See his letter to Trajan, Letter 10.96–97 (online).

31. Trajan: Roman emperor 98–117 CE.

32. Vespasian: Roman emperor 69–79 CE.

of Jesus, or his death.[33] *But he had a servant.*
He enjoyed her immensely. After coitus, she'd
sing him songs she'd composed herself, sung
from the parables of Christ. The emperor asked

this beauty, naked to his bed, to teach these
songs to him, and she did. During the day he
would sing the words to himself. At night,
they bled. In the morning, servants, afraid,

no word to anyone, bleached them to bone.

---

33. Tiberius: Roman emperor 14 CE–37 CE.

WHEN JESUS WRITES WITH HIS FINGER

A Midrash on John 8:1–11

God's enemies, although many
worship them as God's friends,
bring me forward, adulteress,
and stand me before all these

males secretly salivating. They
say they caught me in the act.
How could they have known this
had each, erection in hand, not

been standing outside my window,
transfixed by the joyous sounds
lovemaking brings? Besides—so
captive were they that they could

not see that I was pleasuring myself.
(A lot of us, like you, enjoy this.)
When Jesus writes with his finger
in the sand, he tells all those who

are holding rocks to hurl them at
me—but only if they are without
sin. I feel each stone strike, hard.
But each holds no pain, no power.[34]

---

34. Power: Greek *dýnamis* (English "dynamo," "dynamite") is a key word in the
Bible, occurring about 450 times, over 100 of which are in the New Testament. Ap-
posite here: the Son of God "was declared to be Son of God with power according to
the spirit of holiness" (Rom 1:4); faith should "rest not on human wisdom but on the
power of God" (1 Cor 2:5); "You were dead through the trespasses and sins in which
you once lived, following the course of this world, following the ruler of the power of
the air, the spirit that is now at work among those who are disobedient" (Eph 2:1–2).

THE TORN FLESH OF ONE JUST[35]

A Midrash on John 19:20

The stars now both transfigure and
emigrate. No, not just at dawn, but
during the night, even at the dread
beginning when shapes equivocate,

then decline—no, not into silence
but into divided noise, the sounds
of clanking metal and swords still
marching through the streets, the

idle chatter of wagon wheels whose
each spoke dreams of being cleansed
of blood only to awaken each day to
new carnage. Resurrection has now

come, and stays, and each of us who
followed and believed has splinters
in his hands, innumerable swellings
that speak in languages—no, not

unknown, but in tongues we fail
to comprehend.[36] When, as we lay in
hiding in refugee rooms, the women
returned from his empty tomb; we

each refused to accept the fact that
half of us, still, held hammers in
our hands while the other half gave
birth to nails with each breath that

---

35. The Torn Flesh of One Just: adapted from "the torn flesh of the just," Howard
Nemerov, "The Iron Characters," in Nemerov, *The Collected Poems* (Chicago: The University of Chicago Press, 1977), 241.

36. In tongues we fail / to comprehend: see Gen 11:1–9; Acts 2:1–4.

denied it was from breathing. No, our
women did not rush to us with salve
and ointment. They, though long past
childbearing,[37] removed their clothing

and, with each of them holding one
of us, they lay in newborn bed and
offered each of us a breast. Their
milk flowing, we refused to drink.

---

37. They, though long past / childbearing: Gen 17:15–17; 21:1–2.

THE MOVIEGOER

A Midrash on Matthew 27:24

In Memoriam Walker Percy, 1916–1990

Coarse complacencies both are and beget
sin. Sin, birthed at home or, now, just
as likely brought home as takeout, asks
nothing of us, yet demands everything.

One young person, as she becomes aware
of these things, asks where the nearest phone
booth is. One of her friends, who saw one
once in an old movie of black and gray

and white, tells her that when one of the
film's criminals, now repenting, flees the
set to find a phone booth to summon the
police, his partners in murder and sin find

him and shoot him dead. As the camera now
zooms in for everyone's close-up, he slumps
against the booth's paned side, his face pressed
hard, distended, against the glass, his hands,

bloodied, streaking and staining a mirror, the
phone still in his hand. Our moviegoing Devil,
now, almost, satisfied, arises from his seat. Both
mimesis and Eichmann of grief, casually he strolls

out of the theater, famined. As he derides each open
mouth, each stare, his newly-sharpened horns pulsate,
his emboldened tail swishes back and forth against
the light. He stops at the now-closed concession

stand. Seeing no one, he calls upon its fallen angels,
afraid behind the counter. *A large drink*, he says, *the
largest you have. Make it whatever most resembles
blood. And also, please, your largest tub of popcorn.*

THEY WEPT

A Midrash on John 19:19

He's dead. Not only murdered, but
crucified. No, the jackdaws over
his head didn't mock him, as the
Romans say. When the birds shat

upon the sign, written in blood-
crucifying language—*Iesous
Nazarensis Rex Iudaeorum*—the
birds, unbeknownst to the Romans,

translated the words, at our God's
request, to Hebrew and Aramaic.[38]
But what did the sign say then?
you ask. It began *Hear, O Israel.*[39]

The rest I couldn't hear because
everyone there, even the soldiers,
startled, ran away—except for
the women. (I was watching from

a distance.)[40] They, unheard of in
women, began to rend and tear
their clothes and throw them to
the ground. When the jackdaws

saw them naked, they stopped.
Instead of tearing into his dead
flesh, they gathered at the foot
of the cross. They—something

38. Iesous / Nazarensis Rex Iudaeorum (INRI): Latin, "Jesus / of Nazareth King of
the Jews."

39. Hear, O Israel: The Shema, Deut 6:4.

40. (I was watching from / a distance.): Matt 27:55//Mark 15:40//Luke 23:49.

never before witnessed—plucked
out all their charcoal feathers, one
by one. Now naked themselves,
wing to women's hands, they wept.

YOUR HUSBAND'S BONES: A FRAGMENT FROM *ACTA HISTORIAE PILATI*, THE LOST *ACTS OF PILATE*

I. Pulcheria and Her Trusted Maiden on Jerusalem's Shores

I stand here on Jerusalem's shores. The
tide rolls in, rolls in, yet never recedes.
And yet, the waters never move beyond
these rocks, plenteous as my husband's

tears when he awakens and finds himself
stranded upon an exiled shore. He will
not be allowed to take with him even
his favorite concubine. He will wonder,

when there, *Was this my wife's doing,
and she dried up too early?* He will ask,
Was it childbirths that did this to me?
No, I will tell him. *Well, what then?*

II. Kneeling Into Water

She rarely went out into the cloacal streets,
and never without a guard, heavily-armed.
She slipped out one time, before the night
watch was about to herald false dawn,

with only her trusted maiden with her (she
made very sure that Pilate would never
touch her, subterfuge and misdirection
both her art and her prison). Terrified, the

maiden asks *Where dare we go? Guards
and night patrols are everywhere.* We're
going, she explains to her, to a certain hill
where, tomorrow, they will crucify three

criminals, not only criminals but wanton
insurrectionists who want my husband's
throne—no, not to seat themselves upon.[41]
They plan to take hammers and axe to

it. *Would they dare? Why would they do
that?* Let's first walk now towards this
city's shore. Do you see the waves? Good.
Watch them. What do you see? *They never*

return to the sea's embrace. Good. Now
look closer. *I see—what can this be?—
ships the size and weight of a child's toy.*
Good. Look closer. *I see bloodstained*

wood and twisted nails. Good, good. Now
look below them. What do you now discern?
She lifts her skirt and kneels into the water.
Dear gods, Lady, I see your husband's bones.

---

41. Insurrectionists: Greek *lēstēs* (pl. *lēstai*). See Matt 27:38//Mark 15:27. See
BDAG, 594a: "robber, highwayman, bandit"; "revolutionary, insurrectionist, guerilla."
Lēstēs does not mean simply, and innocuously, "thief" (KJV: Matt 27:38//Mark 15:27).
In Luke 23:39–43 (NRSV), when Jesus tells a "criminal," "Truly I tell you, today you
will be with me in Paradise," Luke uses *kakourgós*, literally, "evil-doer." In all these
verses, the Latin Vulgate Bible has *latro* (Spanish *ladrón*) "highwayman, robber, ban-
dit." "Insurrection" and "insurrectionist" derive from Latin *insurgo*, "to rise upon, rise
up or to; raise one's self, to rise, mount; to rise, grow in power; to rise up, to rouse or
bestir oneself." See Charlton T. Lewis and Charles Short, *A Latin Dictionary* (Oxford:
Clarendon, 1879, 1975), 972b–972c.
Jesus, like Martin Luther King, Jr., Óscar Romero of El Salvador, and many, many
others, died protesting immoral, violent, rapacious, oppressive, and criminal social,
religious, and political systems. In fact, we can call King, Romero, and thousands of
others *nonviolent* insurrectionists, "those who rise up," freedom fighters. See, among
many, Chad Meyers, *Binding the Strong Man,* Walter Wink's "Power" series, and the
writings and witness of Daniel Berrigan and William Stringfellow. For an ecumenical
spirituality of resistance and peacemaking, see Thomas Merton, "Nhat Hanh is My
Brother," in Merton, *Passion for Peace,* ed. William H. Shannon (New York: Cross-
roads, 1995), 260–262, and Robert H. King, ed., *Thomas Merton and Thich Nhat Hanh:
Engaged Spirituality in an Age of Globalization.*

CAN ONE FLESH BECOME TWO?

A Midrash on Mark 10:1–9

But, Jesus, what if one flesh will
not hold? *What does Moses say?*[42]
You already told us that. What
more can you add? *Only this: that*

certificate of divorce is, as you
know full well, written, incised,
deep into the woman's flesh,[43] *as*
the most derelict herdsman sets

about branding his cattle. The
beasts's human cries, daily, even
by the hour, the minute, seize
hold of heaven, not only heaven's

gold and silvered colonnades, its
ivory- and jewel-inlaid portals and
passageways, but also the squatter
encampments always outside the

eastern gate.[44] *There, unlike within,*
there are no Roman toilets, there
are no Roman baths. Everything
is open sewers and fever's dream.

But, Jesus, you've told us that God's
gates lie wide open, even for those
unredeemed. Do you now deny that?
What I said is true always, as true as

Abba, Father, is LORD *and Creator.*
You're not making any sense. *Good.*
What you need to do now is go out
into my Father's streets. Greet the

42. What does Moses say?: see Deut 24:1–4; Mark 10:3.
43. That / certificate of divorce: Matthew 5:31–32; Deut 24:1–4.
44. The / eastern gate: see Gen 3:24.

first woman that you meet, whether
highborn or low or indifferent. Ask
her: Is there one flesh, or is it two?[45]
As you await her answer, count the

doves nesting quiet in her raven hair,
the resting leopard draped about her
unbowed neck, the newborn lamb that
now sleeps, unafraid, upon her loins.

45. Is there one flesh, or is it two?: Matt 1:12, 19; Mark 10:1–9.

THE LORD'S OWN LANDSCAPE:
A FAITHFUL DISCIPLE REFLECTS

A Midrash on John 19:1,
Mark 15:15, Matthew 27:26

The bitter longing that I feel
is something I cannot explain.
But then, I have to try, day
by day, sometimes each hour.

Grief can be counterfeit coin
given when you mean despair,
despair an open wound seeking
poultice and then, joined, repair,

repair a movement that, healed,
will search out others to heal.
When healing, joined, finds its
way home at last, fear will end.

Here in my room, I count, with
Adonai's touch, the lesions along
my back: each scar, still, speaks
Latin, but I no longer obey them.

Each time they questioned me
they asked *Where is this messiah
of yours?* Later they demanded
the whereabouts of Apostle Paul.

Each time I pretended ignorance.
Each time one of them flogged
another welt across my back.[46] I
bear the Lord's own landscape.[47]

46. Each time one of them flogged / another welt across my back: see Matt 24:9;
flogging or other torture could precede crucifixion.

47. I / bear the Lord's own landscape: Matt 10:38; Mark 15:21; 16:24.

WHEN ANGELS FALL

A Midrash on John 20:19–22

I was almost seventy when
I died, an old man, at the
turn of the century, though
we had not yet learned to

count years by hundreds.
I was born the day he died
nailed to that cross outside
her skin. My mother vowed

to follow him into his grave,
then beyond. My father had
fled, never to return to our
beliefs, our hard-won lack

of indifference. It is rarely
fear that effaces us, as most
think, but our showing no
concern as, year after year,

seeds resurrect and birds
return with gifts from lands
we refuse to venture into.[48]
When I was in her womb,

she saw our risen Lord pass
through a wall. Although you
may not believe me, I too saw
it. The Temple didn't quake,

no fracture, nor convulsion,
no near-distemper.[49] What took
place there, some twenty can,
I swear, attest to: the bread

48. Gifts: Greek *cháris* means both "gift" and "grace," and is cognate with *chará*, "joy."
49. The Temple didn't quake: Isa 6:1–5; Matt 27:51.

30

on the table became—no,
not the Lord's body, as now;
we saw the wine birthed into—
no, not his dying blood. No,

but then, those who dare love
and those who bless became
angels. No, not only that once.
We now watch them marshal

mid-air, to defend.[50] But they
have to retreat. The onslaught
of our demons is so very great
that angels fall dead at our feet.

50. Mid-air: 1 Thess 4:17.

THIRD EYE BLIND: AN ALTERNATIVE TRADITION IN ARAMAIC RECENTLY DISCOVERED NEAR QUMRAN[51]

A Midrash on 1 Samuel 17

Goliath lies, third eye blind,
the stone fracturing his skull.
Not dead. His Philistine army
has fled. David's troops now

draw near. *Off with his head!*
Off with his head! The cries
mount like carrion birds ever-
ascending, each with its flesh.

But David pauses. He kneels.
He cradles Goliath's head in
his lap. Tears. He now kisses
the bloodspill. It tastes like the

finest wine. He orders his men
to carry this Philistine back
to their camp. All the camp
followers, afraid of the battle

and its certain defeats, have
fled. Even David's concubine.
Amused, he orders that her bed
and his be brought together.

---

51. Qumran: an archaeological site in the West Bank, located atop a dry marl pla-
teau about 1.5 km (1 mi) from the northwestern shore of the Dead Sea, most likely the
home of the Essenes, an ascetic separatist Jewish group. The Hellenistic period settle-
ment, constructed during the reign of John Hyrcanus (164–134 BCE) or somewhat
later, was occupied most of the time until 68 CE and was destroyed by the Romans,
possibly as late as 73. It is best known as the settlement nearest to the Qumran Caves
where the Dead Sea Scrolls (fourth-c. BCE–first-c. CE) were discovered in 1946–47
and 1956.

His soldiers lay Goliath on both.
David asks them to withdraw. He
covers the fallen warrior. Weary,
he lays his clothing on the ground

and, spent, falls to sleep on them.

THE QUICK AND THE DEAD[52]

A Midrash on Luke 24:13–42

The transparencies of sin
are opaque to the one who
sins, glass blackened that
now awaits its own air raid.

When, against all odds but
those of God, Judas awakens
resurrected from among our
dead, derogatory taunts from

crucifixion grandstands still
hollow into him. He visits the
empty tomb. He and Jesus sit
together, silently comparing
wounds.

Dawn arises, fingers
neither rosy nor encorpsed.[53]
The women find the tomb
empty, Judas and Jesus now
walking together the road to
Emmaus. There, flighted
disciples realize that Jesus
is now available to them in
this breaking of the bread.[54]
Others refuse to believe.

52. The Quick and the Dead: an English phrase originating in William Tyndale's English translation of the New Testament (1526): "I testifie therfore before god and before the lorde Iesu Christ which shall iudge quicke and deed at his aperynge [appearing] in his kingdom" [2 Tim 4:1]. Thomas Cranmer used the phrase in his translation of the Nicene Creed and Apostles' Creed for the first Book of Common Prayer (1549), still used in the 1928 American edition. After Cranmer, both Shakespeare, in Hamlet (1603), and the King James Bible (1611) used the phrase.

53. Dawn arises, fingers / . . . rosy: rosy-fingered dawn, Odyssey 8.1.

54. This breaking of the bread: Matt 26:26–30//Mark 14:22–25//Luke 22:14–30; 24:30–34.

So he tells them that Judas,
though to them a traitor, is
in each morsel, each drop,
now forgiving their sins.

WHAT FORGIVENESS I HAVE FOUND:
THE BELOVED DISCIPLE IN DIALOGUE

A Midrash on John 14:15–27

In Memoriam the Six Million
Yom HaShoah, May 1–2, 2019.
We will not forget.

What forgiveness I have found
is that of burnt flesh. *But—you*
tell us in your Gospel that Jesus
still promises us God's Paraclete.[55]

Yes, I did. I mean, he did. Does.
But my Advocate, my Comforter,
weighed down by blood-soaked
wings, collapses into carnage, its

gore and offense, that within me.
How is this possible? You're his
Beloved,[56] *the one who he loved the*
most. Yes, that's what I believed.

I mean *said.* But my outrage was
so fierce, a holocaust centuries in
its height.[57] Am I now supposed to
apologize? They, *the Jews,* ran us

---

55. Paraclete, Greek *paráklētos*: the word occurs in the NT only in John 14:16, 26; 15:26; 16:7. "One who appears on another's behalf, mediator, intercessor, helper" (BDAG 766a–766b). "Advocate" and "Comforter" are two possible translations.

56. Beloved: John 13:23; 19:26; 21:7; 21:20.

57. Holocaust: Greek *holókautos*, "completely burned"; see Gen 8:20, 22; Exod 18:12; 20:21; among many. For the Holocaust of World War II, Jews mostly use "Shoah," "Catastrophe."

out of the synagogue.[58] They beat us
with staves, prodded us with those
pitchforks they employed to separate
wheat from its tares.[59] The Jews even

knotted our names onto a list that the
Jews guarding the Temple held tight
in their hands. They wouldn't let us
enter even the porch and portico of

those Gentiles.[60] But—Jesus still, still,
blames *me*! *Me*! How was I supposed
to know the Gentiles would use my
words to kill six million of us? How?

58. The Jews: see John 5:9b–18, among many (too many). In John, "the Jews" are clearly enemies; even Jesus in John's Gospel, ahistorically, uses the words. Many scholars think that John's sect of Jewish-Christians either left their synagogue, or were expelled. See James D. G. Dunn, *The Parting of the Ways*.

59. Wheat and tares: Matt: 13:24–30; in v. 25 the NRSV uses "weeds," the KJV "tares."

60. Porch and portico: non-Jews could visit only the outer edge of the Temple precinct, the Court of the Gentiles.

EACH FACE, DISAPPOINTED

A Midrash on Amos 8:6

*To Gary, who first taught me
how to live out social justice*

Satan has diminished more foes than
he can count on resplendent fingers
and toes. Arrayed, he now admires
the nail polish on each of his twenty

angels. He summons Isaiah. Isaiah
refuses a sound. Next in line is Amos
of Tekoa.[61] He now prophesies: *I speak
about Israel and the poor being sold*

for the price of a worn pair of sandals.[62]
Satan now rejoices: *Bring me all those
who do this!* When they arrive, Satan
searches each face, and is disappointed.

61. Amos / of Tekoa: see Amos 1:1.

62. I speak / about Israel and the poor being sold / for the price of a worn pair of sandals: see Amos 8:4–6. Although the prophet Amos (eighth-c. BCE) was from Judah, the southern kingdom, he prophesied about the sins of the northern kingdom, Israel, which fell to the Assyrians in 722 BCE.

MARY MAGDALENE AS SHE WALKS

A Midrash on Matthew 27:27–37
and the Coptic *Gospel of Mary*[63]

He foreshadows himself as he
walks. So does she. She holds his
hand as together they tread the
Via Golgotha, this bastard child

of Way and Skull.[64] She now sees
not a carrion bird, foreshadowing
both, but a simpler being,[65] sparrow
or pigeon, one of God's creations

not in need of healing, searching
the city's trash heaps for a sign
of hope. Mary, once of Magdala,[66]
who will sit opposite the tomb,[67]

sees this, and feels, not the hand
sustaining hers, sweat-stained,
bloody, but the field not far from
her seaside home in childhood,

63. The Coptic *Gospel of Mary*: originally in Greek, surviving in Coptic (late Egyptian), the *Gospel of Mary* "represents the only extant early Christian gospel ascribed to a woman. It gives an account of a postresurrection appearance of the Savior to the disciples . . . After he departs, however, instead of going out joyfully, the disciples are weeping, frightened that what happened to him might happen to them—all, that is, except Mary. She steps in to comfort the other apostles and leads them into a discussion of the Savior's teachings." See Karen L. King, "The Gospel of Mary with the Greek Gospel of Mary," in Marvin Meyer, ed., *The Nag Hammadi Scriptures* (New York: HarperOne, 2007), 737–47; 737.

64. Golgotha: Calvary, or Golgotha, in Hebrew *gwlgwlt'*, transliterated into Greek as *golgothâ*, was, according to the Gospels, a site immediately outside Jerusalem's walls where Jesus was crucified. Matt 27:33, Mark 15:22, and John 19:17 translate the term as "place of [the] skull," *kraníou tópos*, in Latin *calvariæ locus*, from which the English word *Calvary* derives.

65. A simpler being, sparrow / or pigeon, one of God's creations: Ps 84:31; Matt 10:29–31//Luke 12:6–7.

66. Magdala was on the shore of the Sea of Galilee, whose region figures prominently in Jesus' ministry (Matt 4:18; Mark 1:16; 3:7).

67. Who will sit opposite the tomb: Matt 27:61.

sere in winter, God's own desires
in spring and summer. She sees
now what she saw once, and only
once: in a harvest field a lamb.

No, there is no lion, as Prophet
Isaiah prophesies,[68] nor shepherd,
as her Jesus is fond of teaching.[69]
No, the lamb is itself, and healing.

68 As Prophet / Isaiah prophesies: see Isa 11:6–9.
69. As her Jesus is fond of teaching: John 10:11.

PSALTERY: AN EARLY MONK, ONCE DESPONDENT, BY THE SIDE OF THE ROAD

A Midrash on Matthew 5:27–28

I once could pray demons to ascension,
but no more. Demons: a fellow ascetic
says, unsolicited, that all demoniacs have
crawled inside me.[70] Because I think about

a cup—or two—of wine, or the shape of
a woman's breast, a young woman I once
saw bathing beside a stream. The sponge
she bathed with was, I imagined, me, and

I drank like wine each drop that fell from
her beauty. But he, as usual, has it wrong:
these demons—my doubles, my brothers—
have not crept and absconded in;[71] they,

vaulting and leaping, welcome passage
out, where, in sunlight, they cover their
eyes. Darkness has been for them both
mother and widow. They now, together,

---

70. All demoniacs have / crawled inside me, because I think about . . . the shape of / a woman's breast: the saying by Jesus in Matt 5:27–30 begins with "You have heard that it was said, 'You shall not commit adultery.' But I say to you that everyone who looks at a woman with lust has already committed adultery with her in his heart." In Matthew this is one of six sayings, following the Beatitudes and "Do not think that I have come to abolish the law or the prophets; I have come not to abolish but to fulfill" (5:17). Jesus here, as Matthew's new Moses, "rewrites" (and "re-canonizes") Torah passages. From a historical-critical perspective, the six are Christological statements of Jesus as the new Moses; they are unique to Matthew, part of his "new Moses" theme. Jesus often defends divorced women who could well be without resources or recourse; see Matt 5:31–32; 19:7–9//Mark 10:2–12//Luke 16:18.

71. My doubles, my brothers: see Charles Baudelaire, "Au lecteur," "To the Reader": *mon semblable, mon frère.*

41

to my friend's surprise, begin to sing. My
dear monastic brother drops to his knees,
rejoices, and, now stumbling upright,
hurries to the church. He finds that all

lepers, cleansed, sing psalms with me.

THE PRESENCE OF THE LORD

A Midrash on a Recently-Discovered
Passage from a Lost Gospel

Archbishop Theophilus to a female Roman
aristocrat, pilgrim to the monks of Egypt:
"Do you not know that you are a woman?
And that because of women the Enemy
wages war against the saints?"[72]

Once, returning from Magdala,
Jesus sat down on a stone by
the side of the road, exhausted.[73]

After his disciples had left
to ask for food and shelter in
the next village,[74] he watched

each passerby for the Presence
of the LORD.[75] He watched and
waited. A Roman soldier,

spear in hand, sword at his
side, looked at him, not with
the usual derision but with

gentleness and compassion. Was
this because of the camp-follower
at his side, her head uncovered,

---

72. Archbishop Theophilus: Alphabetical *Apophthegmata Patrum*, the *Sayings of the Desert Fathers and Mothers*, Arsenius 28 (my translation); see n. 19 in the Author's Note, p. xxi. Theophilus was Archbishop of Alexandria from 385 to 412.

73. Magdala: see n. 66.

74. After his disciples had left / to ask for food and shelter in / the next village: Matt 10:9–11.

75. Presence: Hebrew *Shekinah*, in rabbinic literature the Divine Presence of God, generally represented, as with Greek *Sophia*, as feminine.

her breasts nearly so? She was
Samaritan, the lowest of God's
low, forsaken, yet she smiled

at him, his mother's embrace:
she held him in her arms and
brought him as close to God as

the womb now his. He awaits
the disciples's return. An oxcart
clip-clops by. When the oxen

see him, they stop. No matter
what the driver does, even with
shouts and lashes, they refuse

to move. The driver curses at
them in Samaritan, Aramaic, and,
with Torah the LORD gave Moses,

Hebrew.[76] But the oxen do not move.
Jesus gets up, soothes the driver,
and, patting the oxen on shoulder

and flank, walks around them to
the back of the cart. When he sees
the posts and their crossbeams,[77]

he has a vision: all Jerusalem has
now gathered at Golgotha,[78] even
women and children.[79] When he's

76. Torah: "Torah" can mean the Five Books of Moses (Genesis–Deuteronomy),
the Pentateuch; and, more broadly, "teaching, instruction," and "law."

77. When he sees / the posts and their crossbeams: see Matt 27:32//Mark 15:21//
Luke 23:26.

78. Golgotha: see n. 64.

79. All Jerusalem . . . , even / women and children: the Gospels frequently use
"everyone," "all the city," and "the whole town" as narrative devices for emphasis; see,
among many, Matt 8:34; 13:2.

44

brought forth, naked, his blood
being collected by paupers and
urchins who dream of shekels,

he asks the oxen, and the oxen's
LORD, to bless and sanctify him.
He now sees the camp-follower

not as a woman he would like to
touch, but as Eve, pursued by the
whips of uncomprehending men.

CROWN OF THORNS: PONTIUS PILATE'S SOLILOQUY AS HE SITS BEFORE JESUS, CIRCA 30 CE

A Midrash on John 18:28—19:16

This Iudeus (he spits, then laughs).[80]

He will spike himself to a cross,
not by my command but due to
some Judean wetdream they call
—what was that again, in that

unintelligible babble of theirs—
Meshiach?[81] How does one even
pronounce that, with its spit-
addled stutter at the bitter end?

Anointed, that's it. Ol' Haruspex,[82]
that stale bread not even birds eat,
tells me they will proclaim, some
day years from now, with peasant

pride, that he was born in some
filthy stable reeking of urine and
donkey shit.[83] It is *I—I* am a proud
equestrian,[84] of sacred Pontii line:

we are Samnite, a very ancient
peoples, suckled by the same she-
wolf's teats that nourished Romulus,
Rome's sacred eponymous founder.

---

80 Iudeus: Latin for "Judean."

81. Meshiach: "Messiah," the anointed one; *Christós* in Greek.

82. Haruspex, pl. haruspices: the word is Indo-European in origin (Sanskrit *hirâ*, "entrails"). A haruspex was a diviner among the Etruscans who foretold future events from the inspection of the entrails of animals. The Romans adopted the practice from the Etruscans.

83. Born in some / filthy stable: Luke 2:6–7.

84. Equestrian: *equites* (plural of Latin *eques*, from *equus*, "horse") constituted the second of the property-based classes of ancient Rome, ranking below the senatorial class. A member of the equestrian order was known as an *eques*.

And yet. Here I have to sit, in this
Judean shithole, adjudicating some
peasant—a bastard yet!—who may,
in fact, have done nothing wrong.[85]

I would now like to look under the
loincloth that our noble guards have
prudently left on him. He reeks. I
would like to find out what the hell

this so-called *circumcision* is—we
have given a very fine Latin word
to their indecent, barbarian, outrage![86]
One more of their superstitious rites.[87]

They say that it provides better sex.
What we Romans could teach *them*!
But, where was I? Oh yes. Sitting on
this judgment bench judging—what?

This beaten-down man has the gall,
has the *temerity*—the *audacity*—to
look me in the eyes. I am *patrician*!
But—why do I see in his own a long

dais where all of my belovèd Pontii
stand, noble Carian statues all? Why
do they all—each one—now look to
me for what judgment I will render

---

85. Bastard: see n. 112.

86. Circumcision: Gen 17:9–14; Lev 12:3; Luke 1:59. Latin *circumcido* means "cut around, cut, clip, trim."

87. Superstitious rites: Pliny the Younger, *Epistulae* 10.96 ("Pliny the Younger—Ancient Rome—Classical Literature" online), calls Christianity a "depraved and excessive superstition." Latin *superstitio*: "excessive fear of the gods, unreasonable religious belief, superstition (different from *religio*, a proper, reasonable awe of the gods)" (Lewis and Short, *A Latin Dictionary*, 1809c).

here? A wearied six or seven years
from now, Haruspex has prophesied,
I will trace each year as numerals on
a tomb's fat ass. I—I—summarily

summoned now back to Rome for . . .
killing a bunch of Galileans? Even
their pig-herding near-relatives abhor
them![88] That whoreson Marcellus, I hear,

son of a whore like this soon-crucified
savior of theirs, will pick up the gold
reigns that I will drop here. It is *I* who
have transfigured mud into precious

stone![89] And yet—before I leave here I
will bathe my reins in insurrectionist
blood,[90] challenging Marcellus,[91] calling
on everyone to find one knock-kneed

nag here that will dare draw near to
haul my bones off into oblivion. I
know, and they do not, that when I
arrive there a crown awaits me. But—

what does Haruspex mean as he says,
in his obsequious way, that it will come
from divine Caesar's shithouse[92] to my
bed of sharpened bones, crowned with

thorns?[93]

88. Pig-herding near-relatives: see Luke 15:14–15.

89. It is *I* who / have transfigured mud into precious / stone!: see John 2:1–11; Matt 24:2//Mark 13:2//Luke 21:6.

90. Insurrectionist: see n. 41.

91. Marcellus: Pilate's successor, he was Roman Prefect of Judea from c. 36–37.

92. Divine Caesar: beginning with Caesar Augustus, Roman emperors, originally at their death, later while living, were deified: Greek *apothéosis*, English "apotheosis." See n. 13.

93. Crowned with / thorns: see Matt 27:28–29//Mark 15:17//John 19:2.

BROKEN, YET SACRED

A Midrash on Qur'ān 2:34, 7:12, and 18:51

Bismillāhi r-raḥmāni r-raḥīm[94]

The bending of autumn light
into its sunset arcs long now
towards—both justice,[95] as our
Brother Martin prophesies still,
and towards our repentance.

In the Qur'ān Satan stands
furious after God creates
humankind. God has ordered
all the angels to bow down
before this resplendent new

creation. All then genuflect,
awaiting God's sweet breath.
God waits. One, al-Shaiṭān,[96]
refuses to submit:[97] *All these
are made of dust and wanton*

*dirt! I myself am composed
of fire. Fire magnificent!
The Fire You first breathed
into everything above when
we, and all of heaven, began!*

---

94. *Bismillāhi r-raḥmāni r-raḥīm*: except for sura 9, all the *suras* (chapters) in the Qur'ān begin with this *āyah* ("verse"; "sign"), "In the Name of God, the Merciful, the Compassionate." On "compassion," see n. 129.

95. Justice, as our / Brother Martin shows us still: Martin Luther King, Jr. (1929–1968), "The arc of the moral universe is long, but it bends toward justice," paraphrasing the nineteenth-century Transcendentalist Theodore Parker.

96. Al-Shaiṭān: Arabic for "Satan," a loanword from either Judaism or Christianity (Hebrew *śaṭan*, Greek *satán* and *satanâs*.)

97. Submit: Arabic *islām* (tri-consonant s-l-m) means "submission" to God, but it is cognate with *salaam* (s-l-m), "peace" (Hebrew *shalom*), so the term means the submission to God that brings peace; in a Christian phrase, "the peace that passes all understanding" (Phil 4:7).

The story goes that God threw
Satan onto the earth and never
thought of him again. Satan
now breathed only basest dust,
the debris from coals that will

never find flame. The truth is,
though, that as earth's Satan
stands cowering in a distance
crafted from gore its blood
(all earth's angels, withdrawn

from below, sidle up to God),
God now drops everything
(the angels hear thunder and
earthquake below), and pushes
all the bowing lackeys aside.

Then God runs, as fast as Deity
can, to this belovèd child,[98] and
hugs him, kneeling before this
broken, yet sacred, soul whose
each sin children now bear away.

98. Belovèd child: of Jesus, Greek *agapētós*, the adjectival form of *agápē*, "the qual-
ity of warm regard for and interest in another, esteem, affection, regard, love" (BDAG,
6a). See Matt 3:17//Mark 1:11//Luke 3:22; and Matt 5:9; Mark 9:37; 10:15; among
others.

PASSOVER'S BIRTHRIGHT

A Midrash on Matthew
27:32–56

When Jesus journeyed from
his garden (whether the
first, his mother's womb,
or the last, Gethsemane),

to the astonishment of
all who were following
him, he blessed a flower
in each. As people ask

why he has done this,
clothing Adam's naked
belief with their own, now
in sudden disrepair, they

watch his back, at each
side a Roman soldier,
and shout out after him,
Lord, Master and Savior,

*we will always follow
you!* After these voices
transpose Passover's
birthright, its scars and

expectations, into betrayal,
crows on Golgotha, once
waiting to peck out each
crucified's eyes, begin

their prophetic psaltery,
looking to each for chorus:
*Why are these three dead
now rising, eyes intact?*

HEROD, HIMSELF[99]

A Midrash on Mark 6:14–29

I once ordered an uncomprehending
Jew traitor to do his own beheading.
Herod now looks in each direction
for friend—even an enemy will do.

He sees no one—but himself. This
appearance makes him sick. He puts
his fingers down his throat to end
his nausea, but nothing comes up.

As he watches his Herodias dance,
a bearded head on a platter, he says,
to no one in particular: *Bring me—*
now—the heads of all who begot me!

99. Herod: Herod Antipas; see n. 24.

AN INDIFFERENT MIRROR: THE DIALOGUE OF PILATE, A PASSAGE FROM A LOST *ACTS OF PILATE*

Passover, 31 CE, on the First
Anniversary of Jesus' Crucifixion

A Midrash on John 18:28—19:16
and Matthew 27:1–26

What predatory dreams are these?
Pilate thinks as a slave shaves
him before an indifferent mirror.

The mirror still refuses to reply.
Now that you're satisfied, at least
for the moment, let me ask you

about this so-called savior named
Jesus. When I am not here, others
come, obsequious, to stand before

me. *They ask* me *about dreams,*
children, advancement through
the ranks. No one there ever asks

how I *am doing. This Jesus, what*
did he do to cause all that trouble?
Nothing? There is no way that I

will believe that! You asked him
What is truth?[100] *When he gave you*
no answer, you saw only then that

the only way forward to veritas
was to vivisection your plight.
You were startled when all the

---

100. What is truth?: see n. 6.

pain began. From within, the
haruspices found no sign that
could save you.[101] *They lay you*

on a gold-enameled bed. It was
then that one of your servants,
a young woman, still a virgin,

whom you'd long lusted after,[102]
comes quietly into your chamber
as you lie writhing in pain. She

touches your wound. Unafraid, she
prays and performs a Caesarean
section, named after one immortal.[103]

When the babies come forth, she
tells you the future of each leper,
cleansed, each one blind, seeing.[104]

---

101. Haruspices: the plural of *haruspex*; see n. 82.

102. Lusted after: Exod 20:17; Matt 5:27–28. The NRSV's "adultery" in the latter, Greek *porneía* (English "pornography"), is better translated more broadly as "sexual sin."

103. One immortal: see n. 13.

104. Each leper / cleansed, each one blind, now seeing: Matt 8:1–3; 11:5; among many.

DESCENT AND ASCENSION

A Midrash on Luke 10:18

Jesus, watching Satan
now fall like lightning,
looked to the heavens
for the source of that

declination. He could
see all of God's tears,
wrapped in wet prayer
shawls or, propleptic,

giving dew to a crown
of thorns,[105] the earth
with butterflies. In those
days, no one hunted them

with bow and arrow or a
lepidopterist's asphyxiate
net or a shotgun. As light
now begins to unsubscribe

each wing, Jesus weeps.[106]

---

105. Crown of thorns: Matt 27:29; Mark 15:17; John 19:2, 5.
106. Jesus weeps: John 11:35; Luke 19:41.

WE AT GREAT DISTANCE

A Midrash on 2 Samuel 11

We at great distance still
hear maidens mourning, as
those at Troy, the wives at
dead Thermopylae,[107] even the

false tears of Bathsheba for
fallen Uriah. When she and
King David are about to hear
the news, they ignore each

importunate knock as they
consummate their each and
partnered indifference. Did
Uriah, sent to the front lines,

receive the fatal blow through
rib, heart, stomach, or groin?
Neither David nor Bathsheba
cares. When the servant, now

dismissed, closes the door, she
listens in the hallway. When
Bathsheba, once again, reaches
climax, the servant girl, known

as Miriam, quickly retreats down
the resplendent corridor, fearful
of the king's response after his
queen cries out another's name.

---

107. Thermopylae in Greece is where a narrow coastal passage existed in antiquity. It derives its name from its hot sulphur springs. The Hot Gates (English "thermal" and "pylon") is "the place of hot springs" and in Greek mythology is the cavernous entrances to Hades. Thermopylae is known for the battle that took place there in 480 BCE between the Greek forces (notably the Spartans) and the invading Persian forces, a battle commemorated by Simonides in the famous epitaph, "Go tell the Spartans, stranger passing by, / That here obedient to their laws we lie."

DEFINITIONS OF JOY

> A Midrash on Exodus 32
> and Genesis 4:1–10

Jesus, once, in empired Galilee,
inflamed the religious captives,
those long immured in walls of
the Temple's devouring, golden

bricks that God had thrown down,
deficient, from heaven, aiming at,
and yet missing, the golden calf.
Seeing all this, God now repents.

Returning the broken tablets to
Moses, repaired, God, no longer
joyful, leans down to ask him
what the going rate for gold is.

Sorrowed, Moses has no answer.
Broken-hearted, God now sets
out to know once more what joy
is, once more its loss, its absence.

Now coming upon Eve by chance,
the LORD God asks: *What is joy?*
Unsurprised, after what she's been
through, she responds, *No, no, it*

wasn't when I, knowing nothing
of birth, bore Cain, my first. It was
when Cain, Abel now murdered,
crawled back into my unlocked

womb. No, not to be reborn, as
we had feared, but to be stillborn.

CUR DEUS HOMO?:[108]
AN OLD FRIEND OF JOSEPH SPEAKS

A Midrash on Luke 2 and 19

With long-practiced carpentry skills
I've saved a manger from disrepair.[109]
Both past and present know Joseph
as a carpenter. They're both wrong.

I should know. He was a *technítēs*, like
me, but a stonemason: he walked each
day to that Roman city to work—its
name Sepphoris.[110] We walked together.

He never got over not being Yeshua's
father by birth.[111] The stories he heard
about some Panthera[112] stuck in his wrists
and feet like bloodrusted Roman nails.[113]

---

108. Cur Deus Homo: a theological work by Anselm of Canterbury (1033–1109): *Cur Deus Homo, Why [Did] God [Become] Human?*

109. Manger: Luke 2:7.

110. Sepphoris: a village and an archeological site located in the central Galilee region of Israel, 6 kilometers (3.7 mi) north-northwest of Nazareth. The tetrarch, or governor, Herod Antipas (20 BCE–c. 39 CE), proclaimed the city's new name to be *Autocrátoris* ([the city of] "one who has full power, sovereign") and rebuilt it as the "Ornament of the Galilee." Several scholars have suggested that Jesus, while working as an artisan (*technítēs* < *téchnē*, "skill," craft") in Nazareth, may have travelled to Sepphoris for work purposes, possibly with his father and brothers, but this is impossible to verify historically. During his public ministry, Jesus does not seem to have visited Sepphoris, or any other Gentile city, and none of the sayings recorded in the Synoptic Gospels mentions it.

111. Yeshua: Hebrew for "Joshua" and "Jesus"; it means "YHWH's Salvation."

112. Panthera: the name of a soldier said by Celsus to be Jesus' real father and referred to in passages on Jesus in the Talmud. Celsus was a second-c. Greek philosopher and opponent of early Christianity known for *On The True Doctrine* (or: *Discourse, Account, Word*), which survives only in abundant quotations from it in *Contra Celsum*, a refutation written in 248 by Origen of Alexandria.

113. Stuck in his wrists / and feet like bloodrusted Roman nails: see John 20:25, but some think the more likely place for nails physiologically was the wrists.

One day, undisclosed to me, they
moved away: his family, his strange
wife, her even stranger son, long gone.
Some said back to Bethlehem.[114] (Why?

They'd never been there.) Others said
Samaria—but why in Sheol would
anyone go *there*? The majority agreed:
David's Jerusalem. For the Passover?

For Passover. That must've been
the reason. Why else? They barely
had two of Caesar's laureled heads
to knock together.[115] Word came later

that Yeshua had ridden poor into
David's royal city.[116] We heard about
the emperor-to-shekel men in the
Temple, tables tossed, coins dancing

across the oppressors's tiles.[117] (I'd
even pay the Temple tax to see that!)
But then they tried—ha!—mocked
and crucified him. (It's always *they*,

114. Bethlehem: Matthew 2 and Luke 2 have Jesus born in Bethlehem. John 7:2
asks (rhetorically) whether Scripture has it that the "the Messiah is descended from
David and comes from Bethlehem"; see 1 Sam 16:18; 17:12, 58. Many, or most, schol-
ars believe that Jesus' birth in Bethlehem is symbolic, the city of David, whom some
expected to return as the Messiah. The Gospels place Jesus in Nazareth; see Mark 1:24,
among many.

115. They barely / had two of Caesar's laureled heads / to knock together: that
is, Roman coins with Caesar's conquering, even deified (DIVI FILIUS), image on it;
the moneychangers would exchange (idolatrous) Roman coins for Jewish coinage so
worshipers could buy birds, say, for sacrifice. See n. 13.

116. David's royal city: see the beautiful hymn "Once in Royal David's City" (lyrics
and video online).

117. Temple, tables tossed: Matt 21:12//Mark 11:15//John 2:15.

isn't it?) Mary and Joseph, probably
shamed, didn't bring his body home.[118]
Some say the Romans threw it into
Paupers's Field; others are going on

about his disciples bribing the guards,
taking the corpse far from Jerusalem
to bury him in some unclean earth.
Still others talk about some empty

tomb, an angel, and women bearing
spices.[119] This, to me, given everything
I saw in Nazareth, all the words he
spoke in synagogue, is most plausible.[120]

118. Mary and Joseph, probably / shamed, didn't bring his body home: sociologi-
cally and anthropologically, the society of Jesus' time was an honor-shame society.

119. Women bearing / spices: Mark 16:1//Luke 23:56//John 19:40.

120. All the words he / spoke in synagogue: Luke 4:11–30.

YOUR FORGIVENESS: DURING THE FINAL DAYS OF MASADA PETER REFLECTS[121]

A Midrash on Matthew 26:34–35, 69–75

I don't know where you went. And
I don't believe the fables that others
are telling us. But with each breath
I take I hear malnourished roosters

crowing. Lord, can you hear them?
They're speaking in tongues,[122] some
of them yours, some of them Herod's,
these words that now have meaning.

You ask me a question. Yes, Lord,
they do still build crosses. I'm an
old man now. No, the stories about
my prophesying in Rome, then being

crucified upside down, are not true.
I'm here, now, at Masada; it's forty
years after you left us. The Sicarii
roast traitors over our open flames.[123]

I know. I will die soon. The Romans
are building ramparts up to us. We've
each gone to where we will leap. Each
nightfall, after our enemies cease, our

---

121. Masada: an ancient fortification in the Southern District of Israel situated atop an isolated rock plateau, akin to a mesa. It is located on the eastern edge of the Judean Desert, overlooking the Dead Sea, 20 km (12 mi) east of Arad. Herod the Great (c. 74–c. 4 BCE) built two palaces for himself on the mountain and fortified Masada between 37 and 31 BCE. According to Josephus (*Jewish War* 7.275–406), the siege of Masada by Roman troops at the end of the First Jewish–Roman War ended in the mass suicide of 960 people, the Sicarii rebels and their families who were hiding there.

122. They're speaking in tongues: see 1 Cor 12:4–11.

123. The Sicarii: see n. 11.

leaders, Gabriel and Michael, and the
hosts of God's angels, work all night
to shovel away what Pilate's ghost is
still commandeering. But they fail.

Soon, the Roman soldiers will climb
over God's last fortifications, swords
in their hands. But we will not be
here: the plan, which all of us have

agreed to, is this: all the men, seed of
Moses, Abraham, Isaac, and Jacob,[124] as
the Romans breach the walls of Adonai,
will jump over the precipice into this

martyr's death. The Maccabees await
us.[125] Though afraid, I too will jump with
them.[126] But, unlike the others, I will hold
the one kiss by Judas in the deepest folds

of your clothing.[127] On my way down into
a sanctified death, I will hold on to this
kiss. Before I hit the earth of your hands,
I will ask, and ask again, your forgiveness.

---

124. Seed of / Moses, Abraham, Isaac, and Jacob: see Gen 9:9; 12:7; among many ("seed": KJV; NRSV: "descendants").

125. Maccabees: The Maccabees were a group of Jewish rebel warriors who in the second-century BCE took control of Judea, which at the time was part of the Seleucid (Greek) Empire. After the victory, the Maccabees entered Jerusalem in triumph and ritually cleansed the Temple, reestablishing traditional Jewish worship there and installing Jonathan Maccabee as high priest. The Jewish festival of Hanukkah celebrates the re-dedication of the Temple following Judah Maccabees's victory over the Seleucids. According to Rabbinic tradition, the victorious Maccabees could find only a small jug of oil that had remained uncontaminated by virtue of a seal and, although it contained only enough oil to sustain the Menorah for one day, it miraculously lasted for eight days, by which time they could procure further oil. The song "Light One Candle" by Peter Yarrow and sung by Peter, Paul & Mary vividly tells and contemporizes the story (video online).

126. Though afraid: Matt 26:69–75.

127. The one kiss by Judas: see Luke 22:48, where Jesus says to Judas, "Judas, is it with a kiss that you are betraying [or "handing over," *paradídōmi*] the Son of Man?"

ALL THOSE WITHOUT

A Midrash on Luke 6:20

*With thanks for Jim Wallis and all
those of the Sojourners community*

I've tried—and tried—to sanctify our guilt
with platitudes, the unforgiven homeless on
our streets,[128] our now-annual decline in life
expectancy because of guns, drug overdose,

suicide. I've tried to tell everyone, dead
and living, about God's love for each of
us, of Jesus' compassion, his guts ours,[129]
for the poor and outcast and crippled and

mad and bleeding. I've tried most of all
to tell—convince—myself that we are all
God's chosen, but my efforts fail, again
and again. The truth is—we learn very

slowly—that we below *choose* not to be
chosen. We stand in line, season-ticket
holders, only to discover that all those
without tickets are those who enter first.[130]

128. The unforgiven homeless on / our streets: a common (mis)understanding
in ancient Israel, continuing into Jesus' day, was that those suffering maladies and
misfortunes suffered them because they, or their parents, had sinned, just as many
Americans believe that the homeless have brought their misfortune on themselves.
See John 9:1–12, especially v. 2; Exod 20:25; 34:7. But, for a contradiction of this, see
Jer 31:29 and Ezek 18:2.

129. His guts ours: in biblical Greek, "to have compassion," *splanchnízomai*, has as
its root *splánchna*, "guts." See Matt 18:27; Luke 7:13; Mark 6:34; among many. Thomas
Merton: "There is no wilderness so terrible, so beautiful, so arid and so fruitful as
the wilderness of compassion. It shall become a pool, it shall bud forth and blossom
and rejoice with joy." See Thomas Merton, *Entering the Silence: Becoming a Monk and
Writer,* ed. Jonathan Montaldo (San Francisco: HarperCollins, 1995), 463. In Hebrew,
"compassion" and "mercy" are cognate with "womb" (noun: *raḥămîm*; verbal root:
rḥm).

130. Those who enter first: Matt 20:1–16.

SATAN'S ANGEL

A Midrash

To Stef, dear friend
now at long distance,
who told us a story
he heard at AA

The call came more quickly
than he expected: Sodom lay
in smoldering ruins,[131] as did
Jericho, proleptic.[132] Jerusalem,

too, 586 years before Jesus
dared to walk this our flailing
earth,[133] and seventy years after
his birth.[134] This angel's wings,

though serried and tattered,
fanned not just one but all
the flames, from Eve's Adam
to the furnace where Daniel

walks on coals surrendered.[135]
Fearful, the angel asks *Are*
we, here, nearer an eschaton
even we could not imagine,

a holocaust not of sheep and
goats but now of women, men,
babies, and their still-lactating
mothers?[136] Satan now smiles and

131. Sodom: Gen 19:1–29. On Sodom see n. 161.

132. Jericho: Josh 6.

133. 586 BCE: the destruction of the first Temple.

134. Seventy years after: the fall of the second Temple in 70 CE.

135. Where Daniel / walks on coals surrendered: see Dan 3. The theme there is God's victory over idols and idolaters.

136. Holocaust: Greek *holókautos*, a sacrifice "completely burned"; see Gen 8:20, 22; Exod 18:12; 20:21; among many. For the Holocaust of World War II, Jews mostly

answers very slowly. Choosing
each word carefully, as if it were
a question of marmalade or only
of butter on morning's toast,[137] he

rocks back in his cockcrow chair,[138]
eyes each emolument gracing the
day's table, sighs, and answers in
soft, soothing, whisper: *What do*

you *think?* The fallen angel,
with no answer, heads upstairs
to his lair. But first he stops by
Gehenna's bathroom. Cradling

the .45 that his Lord and Master
gave him on his first birthday, for
an occasion such as this, after he
pisses and washes his hands, he

stands before the sink, finger on
the fiery trigger. He looks deep into
his eyes. Now he aims, and shoots
himself seven times in the mirror.

---

use "Shoah," "Catastrophe."

137. As if it were / a question of marmalade or only / of butter on morning's toast: when I wrote these lines I had in mind Hannah Arendt's "the banality of evil," referring to Adolf Eichmann and the Nazi genociders.

138. Cockcrow: Luke 22:54–62.

THE PROMISED LAND

A Midrash on Exodus 32
and Deuteronomy 34

Egypt, and its slaughtered.[139]
Moses, just down from the
Mount, Commandments
strapped to his back with
fire, yet without consuming.[140]

Even bent, he now pushes
Aaron aside.[141] The story goes
that he then smelts down the
people's golden calf as they
weep and cry out. He listens

to the hideous, and human,
wails of the calf as it enters
God's own slaughterhouse.
Moses knows its pain, so he
plunges his hands into the vat.

Still bent with the weight
of God's eternal suffering,
he prays over the molten
gold and forms a living
calf. God's Decalogue he

deposits with faithful and
faithless friends. The calf—
the faithful calf—he bears
with him to the very end as
he stands on Mount Nebo,[142]
assays the Promised Land.[143]

---

139. Egypt, and its slaughtered: Exod 1:22; 11:1—12:36, especially 11:4–6; Deut 34:1–8.

140. Consuming: see Ps 39:11; Isa 9:18–19; Lam 2:3.

141. He now pushes / Aaron aside: Exod 32:1–6.

142. Mount Nebo: see Deut 34:1–8.

143. Promised Land: Exod 12:25.

BEFORE THE STONES FLY: A SOLILOQUY
BY STEPHEN, THE FIRST MARTYR

A Midrash on Acts 6:8—7:60

I no longer remember anything before
tomorrow. Tomorrow, just as assuredly
as this pagan sun—now our God's—
will move across this our crucified sky,[144]

announcing itself to all, either silently,
or with the sound of Roman chariots
bludgeoning pavement: Stephen has
died. The reports, late and untrustworthy,

say my fellow Judeans murdered me,
me with my Greek-given name, Stephen.
Stéphanos means *crown*.[145] I was born a
Greek, uncircumcised on the eighth day.[146]

But I came to believe, not in gods, but
in this God of the Judeans, and especially
—against all odds—in God's Son, Jesus.
So, you see, when I was held captive,

bound at the city's gates, there were no
Judeans around: all our women were at
home, praying the Lord's Psalter, preparing
spices,[147] waiting for God's ancillary death,

---

144. Pagan sun: Sol Invictus. The Unconquered Sun, whose worship probably
came from Syria, in the later Roman Empire was "the chief imperial and official wor-
ship till Christianity displaced it." See "Sol," *The Oxford Classical Dictionary*, second
ed., N. G. L. Hammond and H. H. Scullard, eds. (Oxford: Clarendon, 1970, 1978),
999a. Emperor Constantine (285–337) was a follower who seemed to have amalgam-
ated its worship to his recently embraced Christianity.

145. Crown: Matt 27:29//Mark 15:17//John 19:2–5; 2 Tim 4:8.

146. Uncircumcised on the eighth day: see Phil 3:4–5.

147. Spices: Mark 16:1//Luke 23:55–56; 24:1//John 19:40.

what devotion, affliction, and desolation will
bring. The men were hiding in underground
sewers we did not yet have. As they emerge,
each manhole bears a disciple's septic name.

With my fellow believers this way, it is now
clear that it will be drunken Romans stoning
me. As a friend, I tell them my name, first in
Greek, and then its Latin transfiguration. The

soldiers will not listen. Herod, unconcerned,
sends orders to search out, seize, and castrate
anyone who dares contradict him.[148] But when
Jesus arose from the dead, no one dared ask

him the cost of discipleship—although, through
a vision, I understand that those who follow us
will.[149] The sun blinds me. The stone-bearers now
arrive. Misreported facts and rumor will have it

that Saul—I mean, Paul—will be there, watching,
hiding himself dark like a runaway slave behind
a Roman pillar. No. Paul and I had already met,
and knew our fates. He told me, in private, that

he, too, soul-bloodied, wanted to know our Christ.
I then prophesied a vision for him on that dust-
inscribed and ill-kempt road to Damascus. Yes,
he asked for more detail. But who would not?

148. Herod: Herod Antipas (20 BCE–39 CE). The verses echo the horrific crime
of Herod the Great (king of Judea from 37–4 BCE) told in Matt 2:13–18, which itself
deliberately echoes Exod 1:15–22.

149. The cost of discipleship: *The Cost of Discipleship* is a book by the Christian
martyr Dietrich Bonhoeffer (1906–1945), a member of the Protestant anti-Nazi Con-
fessing Church (Bekennende Kirche), murdered by the Nazis just days before the end
of World War II.

So I told him that each blood-red spike in dear
Jesus' flesh had, like mine, his name on it. He,
now grieved, turned to go. *Saul, Saul,* I now
befriended his Pharisee back: *Calm down!*[150]

It is not just your *name—it belongs to me, too,
and engenders all our names!* He stopped and
turned around. My words—I never saw this
before—were hovering in the air, between us,

like sacred birds. He held one of them and
said the Shema with it.[151] Neither of us could
ever have anticipated this. He hugged the
words tight, cradled them, into God's thorns.[152]

He plunged each one, bleeding, into his side.[153]

---

150. Saul, Saul: see Acts 9:1–9.

151. Shema (Deut 6:4): "Shema Yisrael, Adonai elohenu, Adonai echad," "Hear, O Israel, the Lord our God, the Lord is one."

152. Thorns: Mark 15:17//John 19:2; 2 Cor 12:7.

153. And plunged each one, bleeding, into his side: see John 19:34; 2 Cor 12:6–7.

GIFT

A Midrash on Genesis 4:1–16

And Eve—only Eve—arises
now from ashes and their dust.[154]
She alone sprinkles herself:
Abel's death, Adam's denial.[155]

Adam, now clothed, brings
her his hairshirt. She tries
it on for size. It's both too
large and too small. She now

fingers it, appraises its shape
and heft. Lifting it carefully
over her head, she bows, and
presents it to Mary, her gift.

154. And Eve . . . arises / now from ashes and their dust: Gen 3:14, 19. See n. 15.

155. She alone sprinkles herself: see Gen 18:27; Num 19:9; Jer 6:26; Matt 11:21//
Luke 10:13.

DONKEY SHIT: A FRAGMENT
FROM A LOST GOSPEL

A Midrash on Luke 10:25–37

The concupiscence of this offaled
ditch. Almost unconscious, my
head blackjacked by brigands,[156]
I see not stars but wan cripples

and beggars. A leper stops, then
extends his hand. Although in
need, I shrink back in horror and
shriek at him *Go away! You, you*

are unclean! He turns and leaves.
(Or did I imagine him?) But wait—
here's a priest—a priest of the
LORD! He pauses. He deliberates.

He withdraws. *Coward!* I exclaim.
But wait! Here comes a son of Levi.[157]
Damn! He, unlike the holy priest—
not even a pause. *My God, my God,*

why have you forsaken me?[158] Soon
night will come. I cannot move. Out
here, jackals will devour me. I give up.
But who is this? A Samaritan. I would

rather die in this ditch of donkey shit!
But he bends down. He slides his arms
beneath my armpits. Now he is lifting
me! *No! I will not go to Mount Gerizim!*[159]

156. Brigands: see n. 41.

157. A son of Levi: Levi was "the eponymous founder of the tribe of Levi, of the priestly Levites, and of all subsequent priestly" groups. See *The Anchor Bible Dictionary*, ed. David Noel Freedman (New York: Doubleday, 1992), IV.294a.

158. My God, my God, why have you forsaken me?: Ps 22:1; Matt 27:46//Mark 15:34.

159. Mount Gerizim: see Deut 11:29; Josh 8:33. In Samaritan tradition, Mount Gerizim is the highest, oldest, and most central mountain in the world. In Religious

A QUESTION

A Midrash on Matthew 8:28–33

"The demons begged Jesus, 'If you cast us
out, send us into the herd of swine.' And he said
to them, 'Go!' So they came out and entered
the swine; and, suddenly, the whole herd rushed
down the steep bank into the sea and perished
in the water."

I wonder: Has anyone ever asked about these
our demons, drowning in the Sea of Tiberias?
Whether they sank, or swam or, antediluvian,
crawled, God's flesh, to question God's image?[160]

Studies terms, it's an axis mundi, a stairway to heaven, from where one ascends to God.
The mountain is sacred to the Samaritans who regard it, rather than Jerusalem's Mount
Zion, as having been the location chosen by God for a holy temple.

160. Image: Gen 1:26–27.

THREE STRANGE ANGELS: TWO DISCIPLES
TALK AFTER THE RESURRECTION

A Midrash on Genesis 18–19 and John 18–19

I. Angels Their Demons

Abraham met these three,
and they, almost raped
in Sodom,[161] the city saw
not only angels but their
demons, the brown shirts
that some wear.[162] Do you
see them, genuflecting,
on our clotheslines? *Yes,*
they are clean, but also
uncertain. In what world
is that possible? God's.
But, I hear, our God's
not through with us yet.[163]

II. Our Disbelief

Yet is a mighty long
time, so much longer
than the adversarial
ditch each will lie in.
But is eachness also
illusion? Only when
you agree to design.
Which is what Jesus

---

161. They, almost raped / in Sodom: in Gen 19:5 the men of Sodom clearly want to have sex with Lot's visitors ("know" in the NRSV reflects a Hebrew euphemism for "have sex," as in our "sleep together"). The men of Sodom want to humiliate the visitors with anal rape, in that culture a horrible offense against hospitality. Breach of hospitality is the "sin of Sodom," especially vis-à-vis Abraham's previous hospitality in Gen 18:1–8.

162. Brown shirts: the *Sturmabteilung* (SA), also called *Braunhemden*, "Brown Shirts," from the color of the uniform, was the Nazi party's original paramilitary and played a significant role in Hitler's rise to power in the 1920s and 1930s.

163. God's not through / with us yet: see Phil 1:6.

didn't do on the cross.
He fought wood and,
to our disbelief, won.

III. The Fall of Jerusalem, 1099

But when our spikes,
what our God creates,
now begin to celebrate,
each soldier, bored at
day's drear end, casts
lots, not only for Jesus'
clothing, but for when

their descendants, some
thousand years hence,[164]
will declare victory, now
consummating our lusts.

IV. Golgotha's Dogs

When Golgotha's dogs,
in Roman armor, begin
to celebrate,[165] even Pilate,
even he, leans forward
on his couch. Taking his
wife's hand, he decrees
that this day forward all
allegiances to gods not
his own will be forthwith
proscribed and, in that
proscription, crucified.

164. Their descendants . . . : the First Crusade, 1095–1099; the Crusaders captured Jerusalem, slaughtered Muslims and Jews, and established the Crusader States and the Kingdom of Jerusalem.

165. Golgotha's Dogs: see n. 64.

V. But

But you ignore Abraham,
and his sacred hospitality.

FINAL ATONEMENT

To Miriam,
Roman historian,
who got me there

In Pompeii, in the summer

of 2017, I was looking at
plaster casts of those who
didn't make it. I couldn't

tell the difference between
slave, freedman, or –woman,
and Pliny the Elder, famous

Roman author, naval and
army commander, natural
philosopher,[166] who, AD 79,

Christ hanging on the cross
fifty years, died in Stabiae
while attempting the rescue

of a friend and his family
by ship from the eruption
of Mount Vesuvius. What

happened then is anyone's
guess. According to these
our sources, he died two,

---

166. Pliny (the Elder): Pliny (23–79 CE) was a Roman author, naturalist, and natural philosopher, a naval and army commander, and a friend of emperor Vespasian. He died in 79 in Stabiae while attempting to rescue a friend and his family by ship from the eruption of Mount Vesuvius, which had already destroyed the cities of Pompeii and Herculaneum. The wind caused by the sixth and largest pyroclastic surge of the volcano's eruption did not allow his ship to leave port, and Pliny may have died during that event.

disparate, deaths.[167] Like
Judas, who either hanged
himself, or had his guts

blow apart.[168] Neither, though,
is true: when the resurrecting
Jesus sees what will take place

in Pompeii, he asks Pliny,
seven years old, to summon
Vesuvius, lurking as always:

Friend Pliny, resurrect Judas. He's
begging me to ask you. Still penitent,
he seeks some final atonement. He,

who will be unharmed by the deadly
smoke, hopes to go to each corpse to
bury the asphyxiated and offer each

burial, before the lava covers them.

167. Two, / disparate, deaths: Roman sources disagree on the nature of Pliny's death.

168. Judas: see Matt 26:14–16; 27:3–10; Luke 22:3–6; John 13:21–30; Acts 1:18.

MAYBE SHIT

A Midrash on Genesis
2:46–49 and Qur'ān 7:11–12

We, like God, are blessed: we
create, we *manufacture* in its
earliest sense,[169] like God taking
dust, or mud, or clay from the

earth and creating *us*. Al-Qur'ān
recites to us that our creation
is from a drop, perhaps a clot,
or a tear.[170] The Qur'ān has no

snake for us to sanctify, as if
light had to have commensurate
darkness,[171] but it has the snake's
identical twin. Both walk upright.

Iblīs, the Devil—the word comes
from Greek *diábolos*—is furious
that he, *he*, consecrated of fire,
has to bow, God's command,

to these, *these* proud caricatures
made of dust or mud or clay
or—who knows?—maybe shit.
He refuses, so God casts him

169. Manufacture: Latin *manus*, "hand," and *factum*, from *facio*, "to make," thus "to make by hand."

170. Al-Qur'ān / recites: God's first word, command, to Muhammad in the Qur'ān, Sura 96:1–5, is "Recite." Al-Qur'ān means "(the) recitation."

171. As if / light had to have commensurate / darkness: See John 1:5. In Religious Studies terms, this is "conflict dualism" where "dualism signifies a permanent distinction between the material and the immaterial, matter and spirit, body and mind (or body and soul), good and evil, or light and darkness [see John 1]. These distinctions are . . . in opposition to monisms, viewpoints that unify everything into a single ultimate reality" (Jonathan Z. Smith, ed., *The HarperCollins Dictionary of Religion* (San Francisco: HarperSanFrancisco, 1995), 325a-b).

out, down to us, his next of
kin. He growls and hollers,
slavers, pisses, bites, and kills;
he beheads birds as he falls.

To his amazement, after we,
terrified, either run from him
or seek embrace, a few—only
a few—ignore him or laugh

in his face. Dog collar in
one hand, pornography in
the other, or heavy bags of
cocaine-flavored Franklins

in one hand and our disdain
for the poor in the other, like
an eagle on old coins seizing
lightning bolts in its talons,

he trawls the streets like some
desperate john. He's here for
the speeches of Senators, of
those in Congress. He observes

Capitol Hill more fiercely lit
than even Hell. He prepares
to worship. But before he can
open the backpack that God

gave him, he suddenly sees
an angel, one of his fellow
jinn, directing traffic in front
of our monuments. He stops.

He stares. No longer able to
bear our sins,[172] he spreads his
wings patched with creosote
and flies, not home, within.

---

172. No longer able to / bear our sins: see 1 Pet 2:24.

WHEN JESUS, CRUCIFIED

A Midrash on John 19:21–22

When Jesus, crucified, leans
down, he sees his mother and
Mary Magdalene and, now, all
his belovèd female followers.

Each offers him her afterbirth.

THE CHILD AT STILLBIRTH

A Midrash on Luke 10:18 by the
Author of the *Gospel of Judas*[173]

I once sang back all of God's dark
angels onto their fiery, resplendent
thrones: once there, they mocked us.

This was both long before and shortly
after Jesus watched Satan fall from
heaven like a flash of lightning. And

yet. Although Jesus would not confirm
it, Satan never hit the earth. Far within
this silence, one of the disciples asks:

But where is he, Lord? Looking now to
his friends for help, he dares continue:
We didn't see any fires conflagrating

from the cedars of Lebanon.[174] *We didn't
hear the Temple shake,*[175] *its foundations
tremble, the dark angels applauding.*

Applause, says Jesus in reply, *especially
Satan's, is always silent. No. It is far
deeper than silence: it owns solitude's*

very soul. Another disciple, dismayed,
shouts out *But Master, what you are
saying not only disparages ours but also*

---

173. *Gospel of Judas*: "The *Gospel of Judas* opens with an incipit that identifies the text as a 'secret revelatory discourse' . . . that Jesus shares with Judas Iscariot shortly before the time of his crucifixion." See Marvin Meyer, "The Gospel of Judas," in Meyer, ed., *The Nag Hammadi Scriptures*, 755.

174. Cedars of Lebanon: see Ps 29:5.

175. The Temple shakes: Matt 27:25//Mark 15:38//Lk 23:45.

God's very soul, which is your own. Jesus
turns to him. *My earthly form, and yours,*[176]
were given birth long before God, against

the Sacred's own wishes, conceived from
Evil. But after our souls long lay at
their Mother's breast, suckling not milk

but blood and water,[177] *my God saw, both*
in the distance and as near as the seams
that ligature together the fingers on our

hands, that light, though always available,
is as rare as the child at stillbirth who can
learn to breathe in both darkness and its

light,[178] *breathing the air of both as its own.*

176. My earthly form, and yours, / were given birth long before God, against / the Sacred's own wishes, conceived from / Evil: in hierarchical Gnostic cosmology, as in the *Gospel of Judas*, there is a Supreme Divinity (Jesus says above: "my God," that is, the true God). A fallen or lesser God, the Demiurge, is the God (or: god) of creation, which is usually evil; thus humans are children of a lesser God, and the material world is at best an impediment to *gnôsis*, knowledge; at worst a dank waylayer cradling a bludgeon on a dark street. Most of the Gnostic works, those from Nag Hammadi in Egypt, are in Meyer, ed., *The Nag Hammadi Scriptures.*

177. Blood and water: John 19:34.

178. Both darkness and its light: see John 1:5. In Religious Studies terms, this is "conflict dualism." See n. 171.

Once Cain: A Dialogue between
God and Eva's First Son

A Midrash on Genesis 4:8

"Now Cain said to his brother
Abel, 'Let's go out to the field.'
While they were in the field, Cain
attacked his brother Abel and
killed him."

"The first human death was murder."
—Elie Wiesel

No, Cain, I won't resurrect
you until you die. *Does
that imply some limitation
on me—or on you?* Let's
discuss this. Let me explain.

When you were but a speck
in Eva's womb, I knew you,[1]
though you will not know
me until after you die. Eva,
Abel dead, implores Adam
to lie with her once again.

But he cannot. No, not will
not; he lies exhausted. But
when he saw you alone in
that bloody field, he knew
only then that all further
procreations were death.

This was the first fall—not Eve and Adam's misunderstanding.[2] Once you lie within my embrace, east of Eden, you will recall that moment when Adam went into Eve, apologizing.

[1] I knew you: Jer 1:5: "Before I formed you in the womb / I knew you, and before you were born / I consecrated you; I appointed you a prophet to the nations."

ONCE ABEL: A DIALOGUE BETWEEN GOD AND EVA'S FIRST SON

A Midrash on Genesis 4:8

"Now Cain said to his brother
Abel, 'Let's go out to the field.'
While they were in the field, Cain
attacked his brother Abel and
killed him."

"The first human death was murder."
—ELIE WIESEL

No, Abel, I won't resurrect
you until you die. *Does
that imply some limitation
on me—or on you?* Let's
discuss this. Let me explain.

When you were but a speck
in Eva's womb, I knew you,[179]
though you will not know
me until after you die. Eva,
Abel dead, implores Adam
to lie with her once again.

But he cannot. No, not will
not; he lies exhausted. But
when he saw you alone in
that bloody field, he knew
only then that all further
procreations were death.

179. I knew you: Jer 1:5: "Before I formed you in the womb / I knew you, and before you were born / I consecrated you; I appointed you a prophet to the nations."

This was the first fall—
not Eve and Adam's mis-
understanding.[180] Once you
lie within my embrace, east
of Eden, you will recall
that moment when Adam
went into Eve, apologizing.

---

180. This was the first fall: the first time the word "sin" appears in the Hebrew Bible is not at Adam and Eve's "fall," but when Cain murders Abel: Gen 4:1–7. "Fall," *píptō*, does not occur in Gen 2–3 (LXX), nor, with regard to Adam and Eve, in the New Testament. In Rom 11:11 Paul uses a related word, *ptaíō*, of the Gentiles.

A GALILEAN'S GRAVE: TWO FEMALE FOLLOWERS OF JESUS TALK AFTER THE RESURRECTION

A Midrash on Luke 24:1–3

You never did tell me how
the stone rolled away from
an empty tomb. Nor did you

tell me why. Since faith
for you is, at least here,
an act of refusal, I will

set myself an interrogatory
chair and sit in it, alone, in
a room with no inquisitor.

What do you have to say
for yourself? Silence is
not mine, she replies. No,

it informs the pre-dawn
when the rock escaped.
What do you mean? The

rock just walked off, of
its own accord? No, it had
sacred help. One follower

(I never got her name), has
stripped off all her clothing.
She believes that if a guard

witnesses her naked he will
think it is the wine that he
drinks to wretched excess.

Or, if more knackered, he
thinks he sees the sculpted
breasts of his enslaved lover,

a lust he assuages when
alone. So he watches this
woman flow past, like the

rivers of his childhood. He
once caught a fish, he now
recalls, with his bare hands.

He opens and then closes
his memories: now he sees
a woman, naked, walking

easily with a king's stone
slung over her back inside
some sort of illicit fishnet.

He hears church bells in the
future ring. *But what does
such rejoicing bring? Even*

*more, what dare Alleluias
sing?* Exhausted, he sits
down and begins to weep.

Now he imagines himself
pilgrim, those who walk
still to each sacred Eleusis.[181]

Can anything good, he asks,
come from Galilean graves?[182]

181. Eleusis: in Attica, Greece, Eleusis was the chief site of the worship of Demeter and Persephone and was the site of the Eleusinian Mysteries, which emphasized the hope of life after death.

182. Can anything good . . . / come from Galilean graves: see John 1:46, where Nathanael says to Philip "Can anything good come out of Nazareth?"

THEN TO GOD'S WOMBS:
SHIMON SPEAKS FROM HIS CROSS[183]

A Midrash on John 19:18

"There they crucified him,
and with him two others,
one on either side, and
Jesus between them."

He probably didn't see me
die, twisted as he was, north,
trying to save all Jerusalem.

I wondered what he could see.
He was being executed like
any waylaying bandit, me.

I had wondered why they had
left the middle post free, with
me on one side, Judas the other.

Maccabeus:[184] I saw it tattooed
on his wrist, not in Aramaic
but in Hebrew, the language

God spoke when he brought
everything into being, even
these crosses we're living on.

When they brought him, like
us, carrying that crossbeam
across his shoulders, he had

183. "Shimon" is "Simon." "Judas" was a very common name in Jesus' day; the Judas of the poem is named after Judas Maccabeus, leader of the Maccabees (1 Macc 2:66, among many), Jewish freedom fighters 200 years earlier. He is a *lēstēs*, a bandit, an insurrectionist; see n. 41.

184. Maccabees: see n. 125.

a crowd. I had no one. His
followers were all women.[185]
I didn't understand that—

at least at first. When I did,
I was so near death that it
looked to me like the sour

wine[186] someone had given him
had mixed with his blood and
was running into the women's

mouths, each one God's womb.[187]

185. His followers / were all women: see Matt 27:55–56//Mark 15:40–41//John
19:25.

186. The sour / wine: Luke 23:36–37.

187. Womb: see n. 129.

À LA RECHERCHE DU TEMPS PERDU:
EN HOMMAGE À EVA[188]

A Midrash on Genesis 3 (October 25, 2019)

To Leonard Cohen, 1934–2016

Some journeys end before they begin.
Like yours. You were no one's garbage
dump, more like the seagulls now here,
beside the ocean, that dive upon it and

withdraw, and then sling down again.
You wore your transgressions and sins
like handcuffs, but you always had the key
interred between gums and the cheek's

interior skin. As the sheriffs or the guards
slowly approached, even before they could
ask, you had opened your mouth to reveal
what was nothing more, and everything less,

than Adam's birth from earth or clay, and
you beside him, not from Adam's coarse rib,
no, but from the Creator's cascading fire
that you prayed with always and always

our own desire. Now that you're no longer
with us, when asked what I best and most
responsibly remember, I want to respond
Your beauty—no, not you who lay fiery

in bed but you as holy and bereft and near
as your own first smile when, alone, you
first understand: the snake, now speaking,
is there not for your desires, but our own.

---

188. À la recherche du temps perdu: a a series of novels by Marcel Proust (1913-
1927): *In Search of Lost Time.*

HOME

A Midrash on Luke 17:20–21

To Thomas Merton,
prophet and poet of God's
interior, our own

I. Home: A Dereliction

I'm not going to keep going within,
into myself.[189] Outwards is hard enough.

II. In Medias Res

But, I ask, do I have this all wrong?
Is outwards by far the easier voyage?
But, I know, and yet usually evade,
this truth: outwards is drinks with

the guys, whose deepest observations
are often the shape of this or that
woman's beauty and, if she's single,
how available is she? We, half-drunken

friends, know exactly what that means.
We giggle, like boys with some new toy.
What's inward waits outside in the cold,
patiently waiting, our designated driver.

189. Within: Greek *entós*. Or "among you, in your midst." The word can mean either or both. Luke 17:20–21: "Once Jesus was asked by the Pharisees when the kingdom of God was coming, and he answered, 'The kingdom of God is not coming with things that can be observed; nor will they say, "Look, here it is!" or "There it is!" For, in fact, the kingdom of God is among [or: within] you.'"

ONCE, IN GOD'S PRESENCE: A FRAGMENT FROM THE ACTA PETRI, THE ACTS OF PETER

A Midrash on Matthew
8:1–4 and 9:20–22

I. Who Here?

Who here, Jesus asks, can
handiwork stars?[190] Who here
can proclaim a leper clean,[191]
or stop an old widow's blood

streaming? I hear your silence.
Silence before the Creator is
always good. Once, in God's
presence, I overheard a scribe

drop his stylus, gladdened,
then appalled, at what God
was saying. Snow on these
Galilean plains is rare, almost

as rare as God's own lightning
over the hills each soul's home.
Home is where the Lord longs
to enter, in silence, in arrears.

II. What Arrears?

What arrears are these? each
disciple begs. Our Master asks
for a cup of wine: he blesses
it, and pours it into his heart.

---

190. Handiwork: a craftsman (*technítēs*), not necessarily a carpenter. See Matt 13:55. See n. 110.

191. A leper clean: Matt 8:1–3; 10:8; among many.

GOD'S OPEN WOUND

A Midrash on Luke 16:19–31

The movies and TV shows
have it all wrong: Lazarus
still lies at the gate; the rich
people still leave the banquet

drunk;[192] men and women laugh,
fondling one another, stepping
over Lazarus. He lies in God's
open wound, hears the sounds

that offal creates as it makes
its way through unclean gutters.
Lazarus looks up: he now sees
a Pharisee armed in arm with

a Sadducee, heading toward the
next celebration and inebriation.
Now he sees himself pinioned to
a cross, with two insurrectionists.[193]

192. The rich people: see Matt 19:24//Mark 10:25//Luke 18:25.
193. Insurrectionists: see n. 41.

AVATARS OF GOD'S WEEPING:
A FOLLOWER OF JESUS, YEARS LATER,
SHARES HER THOUGHTS

A Midrash on Luke 19:28–44

A day before Palm Sunday
I don't know what time
you are. Are you early
or late? Now, near Palm
Sunday, the furthest part
of me watches you ride
King David's sanctified
stallion while Jerusalem,
holding its breath, will
now hold it forever.

                    The
part of me in the middle
distance listens now to
thunder impregnating
Roman skies. The local
authorities summon each
suborned prophet on the
government's payroll. One
spy now tells the governor
to watch—and watch out
for—this our bedraggled
messiah riding in on a
donkey, one his disciples
have stolen. The room
looks at him; they're all
afraid for his sanity. But
the governor now bursts
forth with a hailstorm of
laughter. His guffawing
is infectious. Columns
tremble and quake in
obedience.

The nearest
part of me, in Jerusalem,
watches from a window:
God's thunderstorm now
shatters every disbelief,
each belief. Everyone,
afraid, has fled. The palm
branches now lie forsaken
along the royal highway.
From beneath them scurry
our citizen rats. Now,
from out of the sudden
darkness come starved,
beaten, emaciate dogs,
avatars of God's weeping.

ALL GOD'S CHILDREN

A Midrash on 2 Samuel 11

"More than 50 killed in
Gaza protests as U.S. opens
embassy in Jerusalem."

—*THE WASHINGTON POST*,
MAY 14, 2018 (ONLINE)

The American Embassy is now
in Jerusalem. Beneath our guns
lies King David. The tempting
flesh of Bathsheba is now its
bone. But Uriah's corpse arises
each day, restores his uniform,
and kills as many Palestinians
and Israelis as he can. Then, in
thanks, he kills himself before
he can murder all God's children.

SEMPER IMAGO IMAGINIS: ADAM'S INQUIRIES[194]

A Midrash on Genesis 1–4

With thanksgiving for the witness of Elie Wiesel,
Shoah/Holocaust survivor, a great and powerful
voice for our six million, and for those of us who
will not forget.

Shema, Yisrael, Adonai eloheinu, Adonai echad.

Not image and likeness, no—image
of an image. Why, Creator, did you
create this mirror and hand it to
me? Why not to Eve who, with her

expectant belly, will suckle the
first death, itself the first murder?
A great descendent will say this,[195]
ash, even after fifty years, saying

Kaddish on his tongue, his tongue
a fire that speaks only of victims.
No—that's wrong. Absolutely not
the truth, neither his, nor ours.

But then why, my hand grasping
this mirror, do I keep saying it? I'm
standing—can you see me?—just
inside, east of Eden, which means

---

194. *Semper Imago Imaginis* (Latin): "Always an image of an image." But classical
Latin does not have direct or indirect articles, so with "the" and "an" in English, the
phrase can have many different translations. See Genesis 1:26a.

195. A great descendent: Elie Wiesel (1928–2016), a survivor of the Shoah (Holo-
caust) and author of *Night*. In a film on the Hebrew Bible whose title I don't remember,
Wiesel reminds us that the first human death was a murder.

within this paradise and manacle
you've created for us and, without
consulting us, called good.[196] Where is
Eve? Oh, yes—you've already told

me: east of here, gathering berries.
One of us hunts or gathers, the other
one cooks. Then the hunter-gatherer
cleans up. No, we haven't dared

go *too far* east of here: you warned
us not to—and here, at least, we've
listened. But, I'm worried—where
is she? Your sun will soon set—and

you still haven't explained miracle
to us. I'm now looking beyond this
eastern wall. But, what do I see over
there—*there*—in the sin-shrouded

distance? Even though you asked me
to name all the animals,[197] you didn't
once ask me to name that—*that*!
There, over there! You call it a *city*?

But why is its name Enoch?[198] Who's he?
My grandson? What's that? Oh, look!
Here comes our Eve! But . . . why is
she carrying over her shoulders a goat,

young, first fruits, and unblemished?[199]

---

196. Called good: see Gen 1.

197. You asked me / to name all the animals: Gen 2:19.

198. Enoch: see Gen 4:17: "Cain knew his wife, and she conceived and bore Enoch; and he built a city, and named it Enoch after his son Enoch." The first city is, at least symbolically, the grandchild of murder. The often-confronting wisdom, and its reality, that lie in myth, sacred story.

199. A goat: see Lev 16 on the Day of Atonement.

CAGES: A NEWLY-DISCOVERED FRAGMENT FROM THE *ACTS OF SIMON MAGUS*[200]

A Midrash on Acts 8:9–24

I've captured so many demons
inside myself that I've built
a cage outside for when they
refuse to sleep, either day or

night. The cage is behind my
hovel (people I've healed are
either destitute or cheap).[201] This
morning, the Lord's risen day,

after I've slopped the demons
inside, I go out to the cages
(there are now three of them)
and feed all the offscourings[202]

to these who are, really, my
only friends. The ones inside,
complaining they are always at
not Death's, but Satan's, door,

refuse to leave; they make their
excuses not to talk with me, or
even greet me—my shadow that
now brings light to all darkened

---

200. In Acts, Simon Magus is a villain, one who implicitly asks Peter for forgiveness. In Luke 2:1, however, Magi, the plural of *magus* (NRSV: "wise men," with "astrologers" footnoted) are very important: "In the time of King Herod, after Jesus was born in Bethlehem of Judea, wise men from the East came to Jerusalem, asking, 'Where is the child who has been born king of the Jews?'" The ancient world *assumed* the "supernatural."

201. People I've healed are / either cheap or destitute: see Acts 8:18–24.

202. Offscourings: see 1 Corinthians 4:13 (KJV); NRSV: "We have become like the rubbish of the world, the dregs of all things, to this very day."

hallways, ones not even I know
I have. So, with both maximum
understanding, and its minimal,
I make my way out into these

streets of Samaria, hawking my
thaumaturgic wares,[203] so to speak
(I, at least, am somewhat aware).
It's only now that this guy, Philip,

attacks me, hurling imprecations
at me, most of which (yes, I *am*
bleeding) I laugh at and escape.
Laughing still, I turn my back

and return to my cages (five now).
Even unfed, my demons are always
glad to see me. I now ask each one:
Shall I invite Philip, my newfound

friend, to join us here for dinner?
I'll make us all something special.
They call a council. I wait. *No,* they
say, *He'll refuse to believe in us.*

203. Thaumaturgic, Greek *thaumátourgos*: a wonder-worker. The word doesn't oc-
cur in the NT, but words built on its root, *thaúma*, "wonder, miracle," do: *thaumázō*
("to be extraordinarily impressed or disturbed by something"), and *thaumásios* and
thaumastós ("to be a cause of wonder or worthy of amazement, wonderful, remark-
able, admirable"); BDAG 444a–445a.

PROLOGUE AND ITS AFTERMATH

A Midrash on Genesis 2:4b–3

I. How Far Apart

The unrequited love a sailor brings
to the woman in port whom he pays
is, nevertheless, love, however brief.
The love we walk into church come

a Sunday is, in truth, translucent and
beclouded,[204] their Creator, apophatic.
From the cross and eucharistic table
Jesus squints at us. He leans down,

crucified, reaches out, and touches
the unconsecrated bread and wine.
They turn to dust. Unsurprised, he
leans closer still: he sees now that

the dust is both Eve and Adam[205] as,
after creation, they lie looking up at
the constellations God will not ask
them to name. Yet stars give light

to both. Still, in the dark, Adam
is afraid. But Eve points up: *Those
stars there, see them? They are you,
aroused. And those stars over there—*

*over there, look!—speak to me when
I seek orgasm. How far apart they are!*

204. Translucent and / beclouded: these terms, as well as "apophatic," try to capture something of the theological and mystical understandings in Judaism, Christianity, and Islam: what is kataphatic, "effable," and what is apophatic, "ineffable," about what can, and cannot, be said about the Sacred or God. The title of the anonymous mystical treatise, *The Cloud of Unknowing* (mid-fourteenth c.) gives metaphor to the ineffable. Douglas Adams (1952–2001), author of *The Hitchhiker's Guide to the Galaxy*, puts it memorably: "Let's think the unthinkable, let's do the undoable. Let us prepare to grapple with the ineffable itself, and see if we may not eff it after all."

205. The dust is both Eve and Adam: see n. 15.

II. Why This Distance?

Why this distance, Adam? Adam has
no reply. Dejected, he dresses. Eve
remains naked. Looking in a mirror
that an angel, just given, holds up,

she looks more deeply, Adam standing
behind her. *You know,* she tells him,
*you know, when I first understood that
my breasts were not uniform, one a bit*

*lower—or is one a bit higher?—than
the other, I was intrigued. Aren't you,
Adam, symmetrical?* When he doesn't
answer, she—no, she doesn't dress but

turns herself towards another, Adam's,
mirror. It now speaks of rotted fruit. She
takes hold of it and, in praise, presses it
to her breasts. It's cold but, she quickly

discovers, becomes warmer and warmer—
no, not when Adam, mute, undresses or
she covers herself—only when they both
discover, now east of Eden, everything that

the Serpent, without ego, once suggested.
God now asks them for loincloths in order
to hide his shame, aware, for the first time,
of nakedness, both its prologue and its past.[206]

206. Its prologue and its past: Shakespeare, *The Tempest* II.1, "What's past is prologue."

A SNAKE UPRIGHT

A Midrash on Genesis 2:4b–3:24

To Mary Oliver, requiescat,
January 17, 2019

How many of us stop to think
about a snake walking upright?
But that's what Genesis says
was the rule, not the exception.

Yes, pre-lapsarian, of course.
Genesis, in its course, does not
defame—thus define—him
as Satan, which allows us here

to channel now a new course
(handing the serpent a mirror),
deep, undoubtedly deeper even
than all the honest soteriological

explorations of Saint Augustine,
Saint Thomas Aquinas, Karl
Barth, and so many others (pray
for us now, and at the hours of

their deaths).
        Now that we are
free, free to breathe and imagine,
let's sit down, here, at this lovely
outdoor café, in this city of our

becoming.[207] Let us call the waiter
and order coffee, wine, or beer,
the five of us—you, me, Eve,
Adam, and the serpent sitting—

---

207. In this city of our / becoming: see Matt 24:7–8; Jas 1:18.

and, offering a toast, ask him
Doesn't it worry you that you
will soon lose your opposing
thumb, and, thus, your ability

to point out, and even pluck,
fruit from forbidden trees?
Are you sad, or pissed off
(we would be), that you will

no longer be able to speak
and, thus, contradict God,
who made you upright, and
his version of your story?

THAT GHOST AGAIN: A PROSE POEM AND DRAMATIC MIDRASH ON BARABBAS

A Midrash on Mark 15:6–15; Matt 27:15–26;
Luke 23:13–25; John 18:38—19:16.

To †Marcus Borg, John Dominic Crossan,
†William R. Herzog, Richard A. Horsley, and
†Walter Wink, New Testament scholars.
And to Jeff Russell, magistro amicoque, who first believed in this poem.

Dramatis Personae:

- Barabbas

- Aelius (offstage, non-speaking)

- Jesus (offstage, non-speaking)

"Pray for us sinners, now and at the time of our death."[208]

Barabbas [*sitting on the ground*]: It sure stinks in here. That guy with the runs may as well be called *Shitstorm*. It's even worse in this God-forsaken hole than standing near all those unwashed pilgrim bodies traveling for days and even weeks in Spring's surprise heat. You'd think holy Judea [*spits*] would cleanse them with every step, even wash the mule- and donkey-shit off their sandals and the hems of their travel clothing. Passover garments safely stored where neither moth nor rust destroy—where did I hear that? [*Silence*] But as fellahin who can't (or won't—good for them!) pay their Temple tithes and taxes, they're unclean by definition, like some leper, or a guy without a dick. (Tell me: How would the Temple sycophants, aka police, know that?) So, maybe holy Judea's cleansing powers don't work with them—except, of course, for a price. That's undoubtedly what the priests and their bagmen tell them.

[*He looks around*] God, it's dark here. It's so fucking dark in here. I've always worked outside; I love heat and sun, their sweat that muscles bring. But the occasional guard-torch that passes by only mocks—ha!—mucks—any possibilities of light. No windows, either, so no chance of star-gift or moon-thunder. But why should I complain? Outside there's

208. Pray for us sinners, now and at the time of our death: the conclusion of the "Ave Maria" ("Hail Mary").

104

only unyielding sun-squalor. Hey, maybe, in my captivity, I'm becoming a poet! And a bitter one, at that—like Naomi, who changed her name.[209] The wonder is that I can see to think. I *can*, though, see my thoughts parade and prattle my hour on the stage.[210] At least they can't take my thoughts away from me.

[*In reverie*] I can't believe I snuck into that theater as a young boy; the play was in Greek, by someone, I heard, called *Dramaturge*. Back then I could understand only a few barbarian words here and there.

[*He leaves his reverie*] These Romans—they imagine, with what little imagination they possess, that we're *all* peasants, bumpkins that they for their amusement make pig-ride[211] so they can wager the Caesars burning holes in their purses.[212] Swords always at the ready, as our kids fall off their pigs and land in the mud and pigshit, soldiers guffaw and slap each other on the back and punch each other's arms as they offer another round of basest wine to their emperor, that distant, yet all too proximate, god.[213]

[*Barabbas stands*] I am an insurrectionist—and proud of it.[214] But I'm not a thief, as some, idly gossiping the street, masquerade me. I hear various reports from Aelius. He says his name comes from Greek *helios*, "sun." [*Smiles*] Maybe his parents invented irony. He's the one guard here who has more than a gnat's intelligence. And he appreciates that I can get by in Latin. *And* he hates this shit-filled darkness down here as much as I do.

[*He sits*] He tells me he'll get his mustering-out allotment soon; he'd like to settle in the Peloponnese, he says, where he once garrisoned, grow

209. Like Naomi, who changed her name: in the biblical book Ruth (1:20), Naomi changes her name from Naomi ("pleasantness") to Mara ("bitterness").

210. Pray and prattle my hour: see Shakespeare, *Macbeth* V.5.2381–82: "Life's but a walking shadow, a poor player / that struts and frets his hour upon the stage."

211. Pig-ride: this image comes from an event in Texas. A Muslim group built a mosque on some empty land; on Saturday, Islam's holy day, the farmer next door would hold pig races at the fence dividing their properties. Pork is ḥaram, "forbidden," in Islam.

212. The Caesars burning holes in their purses: see n. 115.

213. That distant, yet all too proximate, god: see n. 13.

214. Insurrectionist: see n. 41.

some grapes and olives and, in the heat of summer, do as the prophet prays: sit under his own vines and lie down under his own fig tree.[215]

Feeling something like friendship for him—this guy who'd take my head off in a second if so commanded; think: Peloponnese—I told him that no one would make him afraid there. I hear from him, far from his fig tree and vines, that word on the street and in the soldiers's quarters has me being part of, or even leading—now, *that's* a joke!—an uprising or insurrection or rebellion—bandits! Those are the words, he says, being bandied about. (I am *so* clever with words! Ha!)

[*He gets up*] Guilty as charged! And proud of it! But murder? Never! I'm not one of those blood-and-dagger guys. What's that strange word— Sicarii?[216] Definitely not Hebrew or Aramaic. I'm still observant enough— *Adonai eloheinu, Adonai echad*—that I honor the Commandment that asks—and enjoins—me not to kill.[217] The Romans do the killing, with swords, then accountants's sheets. Then the bastards blame everything on *us*. The tribute that goes back to Rome, after our disemboweling, then daily gutting here, leaves a trail of blood spatter; armed couriers ride off into an imperial gore-stained sunset that drops viscera and drips bloodstain. Some of us with more than single-syllable words joke—bleakly, I suppose—that all roads leading to Rome from Palestine should be called The Sluices of the Abattoir.

[*He paces*] But now, I hear, they've got some Galilean peasant, same name as me—Jesus—Yeshua—Jesus, son of Mary, whatever that means. Does he have a father—rather than my patronymic, Jesus son of Abbas, son of the Father?[218] I've never seen him, at least in the flesh that Adonai has given us . . .

[*He sits*] Though I did see him—I swear!—in a vision: he was sitting by himself, away from the others, when a raven flew down and landed on his shoulder. Even in here I can hear the necromancers squawking! But then

215. Do as the prophet prays: sit under his own vines and lie down under his own fig tree: see Mic 4:4.

216. Sicarii: see n. 11.

217. Adonai eloheinu, Adonai echad: this is part of the Shema (Deut 6:4): "Hear, O Israel, the Lord our God, the Lord [is] one."

218. My patronymic, Jesus son of Abbas, son of the Father: the name "Barabbas" means "Abba's son," "son of the father." It's likely that the name, and the story, are symbolic. On Jesus' use of "Abba," see Mark 14:36; see also Rom 8:15 and Gal 4:6.

the bird leaned down—I swear!—and this Jesus lifted his head, and they began a spirited conversation. I could make out only occasional words—the blackbird had a very high voice, like a woman's in anger or in heat; Jesus' was more like a low rumble—maybe "mumble" is better—as when you hear from a distance the cartwheels, the movement of conquering troops, on a sun-scorched road . . . And then, of course, since you're no dummy, you head out, as fast as you can, in the opposite direction.

And then I woke up.

[*He stands up*] Why was I sweating? Inside it was cold, subterranean-cutting, as freezing as that ice I saw once: a fellow traveler there told me that in deep cold he was shown Adam's footprints as he left the Garden, now filled in with hail, Adonai's fallen tears.

Aelius came in that one time, before my vision sewered itself like every-thing else in this shithole. From behind his torch, he said in a whisper, so no one would hear him, that he wanted to talk with me about this other Jesus. Coincidence, or fate? Or a pillar of fire?[219] At first I couldn't tell if he was scornful, or smitten. He quickly squatted; he'd been escorting a prisoner, now dead, when he saw "the Nazarene," as some call him, talk-ing with some people.

He wanted to catcall him—stupid Galileans, next-of-kin to the Samari-tans—but something made him stop. My Roman buddy [*shaking his head*] told me this Jesus was excited; he was telling people some nonsense about some "Kingdom of God" where God loves everyone alike; where the Lord's not kept on a leash like a beaten dog ever choked tighter in the inner sanctums of the rich and priestly, paraded about on High Holy Days. It's rumored that his followers sell everything they have and share it—even with the unclean![220] Well, this much is clear: *he's* not bought for a price!

[*He sits*] Aelius told me word for word (he promised) a story—what does this word "parable" mean?—by this Jesus about some guy, some rich parasite sending out invites; stiffed by his friends and retainers, however, he invites *everyone* off the street to his sumptuous banquet. That's harder to imagine, especially here in Jerusalem, than the Romans draping me in

219. Pillar of fire: Exod 13:21.
220. His followers sell everything they have and share it: Acts 4:32.

purple's fine raiment and offering me crown and scepter and license to rape, maim, and kill!

[*Getting up*] But, Aelius said, Jesus got quiet. People began shuffling their feet like sheep milling about in a pen. He wouldn't stop looking at us, said Aelius. Jesus looked sad but—how do I put this?—also deeper than that. Then my guardfriend even choked up—a Roman with emotions!—telling me—a Roman educating a Jew!—all about *chesed*, love and compassion. His pronunciation was laughable! I once heard a teacher explain that Torah begins with *chesed* and ends with *chesed*. Love, compassion, mercy, forgiveness.

"Compassion"—didn't expect to hear from that ghost again. I thought that maybe we'd even obliterated it from our vocabulary, meager as it is, like when the Temple servants come out with buckets of water after the sacrifices and sluice unholy offal into our mouths—which are, the high holy ones've decided, cloacal.

[Pauses] I felt compassion—once—or at least something like it. I saw a Roman boy, accompanied by a slave, brandishing a small wooden sword, stabbing the air at this and that. *So, that's how they train them*, I thought. But then—to my surprise, I admit—I reflected on my own interior violence, the sword that's always encamped in my heart, pushing to come out of my mouth; climbing my ribs, it seems, to get into my battleslaughter hands.

I looked again at the boy and—I know, I know—felt love for him. But then the sword as he waved it about went from shadow into light and lit up, like conflagration, like flames spreading through firestormed trees. It then turned scarlet with blood, and that blood, too, became sewered. Then, despite my efforts, when I looked at the boy, all I felt was revolt, revulsion . . . But now, in here, I have to wonder what—or whom—I was recoiling from.

[*Sitting down again*] I wish I knew what Jesus and that blackbird were saying. I wish I could know what that boy will do when his sword becomes metal. I'd especially like to know what the slave was thinking as he bobbed and weaved and sucked in his gut so he wouldn't get stabbed. Yes, dear Jesus Barabbas, voice whispering to my ear, I know what holy Torah—or at least its armed gatekeepers, its watchdogs—says about soothsayers and night visions. And yes, brother, I know that some have named me *Dreamkeeper*—which sounds, of course, a lot like *Shitsleeper*!

[*He stands*] But it all makes me wonder, nevertheless. One of this Jesus' followers in the cell next door, one of those with the high-falutin' title, la de da—in Greek, moreover, "disciple"—says *this* Jesus, unlike me, speaks with the LORD, Adonai, as *abba*, "father." Why would he do that? It's nowhere in Scripture, at least that *I've* heard. *My* father—that drunk—bludgeoned me with what he thought was love—prostituted, of course, with drink—until, at thirteen, I escaped to Uncle Simeon's. *He* put me to work castrating goats.

[*He sits, exhausted, and leans back against the wall, ignoring the dankness.*] And now Caesar, or at least his lackey, Pilate, has *me* by the balls. [*He laughs; others turn their heads towards him*] Is the rumor true? Aelius says it is. I hear distant keys; maybe that's him coming. That they release one prisoner in honor of the Passover? Never heard of it; maybe it's something new—you know, stroke the beast, wary as you are with half a legion as collateral, so it doesn't bite your balls off.

Aelius says the crowd is calling for *me*. [*Laughs*] Me! [*Laughs again*] One Jesus for another. But . . . if they let me go, that means that this Galilean dies. But isn't that redemption as a roll of the dice? [*Pauses*] I heard something the other day about some trouble in the Temple caused by this guy, turning over tables, scattering money on the Temple's barren ground like seed.[221] Ha! Big-fucking-deal. Even blowing your nose in public, or pissing against a wall, or scratching your balls, is now "insurrection."

[*Pauses; then quietly*] Word has it that one nose-blower, one wall-pisser, and one ball-scratcher will soon be crucified together. [*Sighs*]

[*He stands and paces*] Are they going to ask *me* to choose? Fat chance. But if they did . . . if they did . . . : if I told them to take *me*—though, I repeat, I'm no murderer—to Skull Hill[222] instead of Mary's son, whatever *he's* done, would the light that emanates from Roman swords, Roman spikes, impale only me, my far- and near-sightedness, my too-often-feral heart-failings? Or would it cause all Jerusalem to wither and burn from its heat?

---

221. Scattering money on the Temple's barren ground like seed: Matt 21:12//Mark 11:15//John 2:14–15.

222. Skull Hill: see n. 64.

Part of me, I admit, would like that; [*stops pacing*] would love to witness the imperial and priestly crossbeams that buttress their palaces fall, crash, and flame into ash, burning them into unclean sacrifice. Would it cause this Jesus and all his followers (I hear) to blink and cringe before the sun's adjudications, sheltering their faces, with their arms entombing their eyes?

I don't know. [*Pauses*] I weary not only myself but even these stones, shit-laden as they are. If I could, I'd hammer God's sun to this manacled wall—if it would help, if it would bring me light and free me, and, more importantly, with its warm radiance, end the need for insurrection. *All* insurrection. Yes—*please* believe me—if they let me out of here I will cry "Peace! Peace!" where there is no peace.[223] But *could* there be? If Sol Invictus,[224] or this Jesus, could do that, kneeling before the LORD's second commandment I'd call it, or him, God, whether distant, or nearby, or within.[225]

[*He hears keys rattling*] There, I said it. By doing these things, by following the words of my mouth, the meditations of my heart,[226] I'd give my days to pulling out every imperial spike—no other violence needed—hammered or not, now and forever. Amen. Then all of this, all of it, even this Jesus whom I've met only in vision and in martial words, perhaps especially he, would have been worth it.

Well, look who's here. That ghost again.

---

223. "Peace! Peace!" where there is no peace: Jer 6:13–14; Ezek 13:10.

224. Sol Invictus: see n. 144.

225. Second commandment: Exod 20:4, "You shall not make for yourself an idol, whether in the form of anything that is in heaven above, or that is on the earth beneath, or that is in the water under the earth."

226. The words of my mouth, the meditations of my heart: Ps 19:4.

LACRIMAE RERUM, LACRIMAE GAUDIAE:
CODA & EPITHALAMION

I am now leaving, in absentia
yet present. I ask questions
of Scriptures. Sometimes they
answer. When they don't, they

ask *me*—no, not to surrender,
but to pray ever more slowly.
That I can do, but seldom
without impatience and its

pain: *lacrimae rerum*. But—
lacrimae gaudiae.[227] Joy and
her dear sisters[228] embrace me
more than before: they pick

through offal and bones. When
they arrive, She blesses both
of my sorrows: her truths, and
my fears. In both I now take

comfort. Comfort now draws
near. She bends over each flower
growing inside me. With each

flower's scent and ascent, She
sings: Gloria in Excelsis Deo.[229]

---

227. *Lacrimae rerum*: Virgil, *Aeneid* I.462, sunt lacrimae rerum. Seamus Heaney's translation: "There are tears at the heart of things" ("Virgil's Poetic Influence," BBC broadcast, online). *Lacrimae gaudiae*: tears of joy.

228. She: "joy" in Greek is *chará*, a feminine noun; see Matt 13:20; Luke 1:14; 15:7; among many. It's worth noting that "joy" occurs over 250 times in the Bible. It is cognate with *cháris*, "grace," which occurs over 100 times in the New Testament.

229. Gloria in Excelsis Deo: Latin for "Glory to God in the Highest," dating to the second or third century, sung still in many churches.

Index of Ancient Documents